THE
NEW FOREST
AT WAR

JOHN LEETE

The
History
Press

First published in 2004 by
Sutton Publishing

This anniversary edition first published
in 2009 by The History Press
The Mill, Brimscombe Port,
Stroud, Gloucestershire, GL5 2QG
www.thehistorypress.co.uk

Reprinted 2011, 2012

Title page photograph: On exercise at
Pylewell, *c.* 1942. *(Lord Teynham)*

**British Library Cataloguing in Publication
Data**
A catalogue record for this book is available from
the British Library.

ISBN 978-0-7524-5193-0

Typeset in 10.5/13.5 Plantin.
Typesetting and origination by
The History Press.
Printed and bound in Great Britain by
Marston Book Services Limited, Didcot

*To Rebecca, Maxine and Abigail
and to Michael for the gift of life*

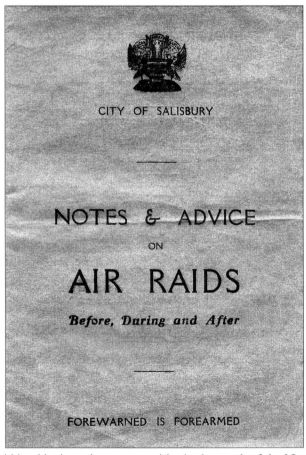

An air raid booklet issued to communities in the north of the New Forest,
close to the city of Salisbury.

Contents

Foreword

by Lord Montagu of Beaulieu

Reminiscing can be an indulgence and a pleasure. Equally, it can bring back regrets and sadness. For the historian, other people's memories are history but, unfortunately, memories fade and the historian has the duty to record our memories for the benefit of future generations. That is why this book is so important and we owe a debt of gratitude to Mr Leete for masterminding the publication. As one of those who was

born and brought up between the wars, we heard the older generation's memories of the First World War, 'the war that was to end all wars'. Little did we know in the short period of twenty-one years the Second World War would break out and that we would experience its impact in so many ways. I must admit that as a boy of fourteen I looked on the outbreak of hostilities with excitement, as I imagined British Spitfires shooting down German Messerschmitts and spent much of my spare time making model planes. As time passed, though, I gradually became aware of the horrors of war. However much we were cheered by the victories of the allies there were dark days. Friends and relations were killed and the future was uncertain.

There were few areas in Britain which were not affected by the war, but London and the south were particularly involved. The geographic position of the New Forest made it a very special place. First of all it played a vital part in defending the south coast from the anticipated invasion by the Nazis from over the Channel. Later on, of course, it became the spearhead for D-Day, which from 1943 saw an ever growing concentration of troops and naval personnel billeted in the forest. Roads were widened for the tanks, anti-submarine barriers built into the Solent and the Beaulieu river packed full of motor torpedo boats and landing craft, and not forgetting the aerodromes: initially Coastal Command Liberators used Beaulieu Aerodrome and later of course came the American and RAF fighter bombers. Today, everywhere one can find relics of the war, old pillboxes, disused runways, redundant jetties and the dock on the Beaulieu river where parts of the Mulberry Harbour were built.

This book is a tribute to those who were involved in, or witnessed, the New Forest at War. We must never forget that many brave men and women left the New Forest never to return.

Although I was only a teenager at the start of the war, I feel very privileged to be sharing my memories with others who lived in the Forest during this period. The personal memories recorded in this book will act as a permanent reminder to the younger generation of the Forest in the Second World War.

Introduction

by Julian Lewis MP

The New Forest in Hampshire is one of this country's great treasures. Rich in social history, the Forest's woodlands, wide open spaces and abundance of wildlife and stunning views attract millions of visitors every year.

It has been an inspiration to generations of artists, writers, photographers and poets. The Forest gives pleasure to all those who live and work within its boundaries.

To many it appears to have changed little over the years; however, within living memory, the Forest was pivotal in the great campaign Operation Overlord. For it was here that thousands of troops were stationed in readiness for D-Day: here, off the Forest coastline, a great armada of ships was assembled; and here, twelve airfields were constructed from which our aircraft flew sorties before and during the D-Day campaign.

Keen observers will recognise remains of the military occupation right across the Forest, from the Waterside in the east to the Avon Valley in the west. For example, pieces of concrete, pillboxes, airfield tracking, derelict buildings, all legacies of those far off but desperate days can be found here.

Many of the area's manor houses and estates were requisitioned and used by both the Allied and British Armed Services and we are able to visit some of those locations today.

Now it is to those who lived in and knew the area that we turn to for the real story of the New Forest at War. This is a unique story, which will be of interest to all those who live in, work in and visit the Forest.

1944–2009
— 65th Anniversary of D-Day —

13 March 1939

AT THE COURT OF SWAINMOTE AND ATTACHMENT FOR THE NEW FOREST VERDERERS HALL, KINGS HOUSE
George Meyrick (Major Sir), Chairman

Military Manoeuvres
The Clerk stated that there were 'several applications in this connection but up to the present no definite information from the War Office had been given but already some of the Officers had interviewed him regarding the sites and areas to be asked for. There would be many troops in the Forest if the manoeuvres take place. The Official Verderer* stated that he had received an application from the Blues (Cavalry) but in view of the various applications received and of the number of troops coming into the Forest it was doubtful there would be room for the Cavalry.'

Sites for Anti-Aircraft Guns
Mr Young, Deputy Surveyor – stated that 'applications had been made regarding sites for AA guns and there was suggested the question of an emergency in this direction and also a demand for huts to be put up. The Verderers decided that they would not raise any objection.'

* The area has its own, quite unique, body of representatives, known as Verderers. They also act in the capacity of a pseudo 'police force' to safeguard the interests of the Forest and the commoners. The place where they meet to discuss and make policy is known as the Verderers Court and this is situated in Lyndhurst, the county town of the Forest.

1

The Dawn of War

The New Forest, rich in natural and social history, is one of Europe's major tourist destinations with some 20 million visitors every year enjoying the unique mix of wildlife, woodlands, picture-book towns and villages, friendly people and vast open spaces. Recreational activities of all sorts can be enjoyed here from riding and fishing to walking and camping. The poet John Wise wrote 'The best advice which I can give to see the Forest is to follow the course of one of the streams, to make it your friend and companion and to go wherever it goes. It will be sure to take you through the greenest valleys and past the thickest woods and under the largest trees. So step along with it for it never goes out of its way, but in search of some fresh beauty.'

The New Forest (presently covering an area of over 200 square miles) stretches from Christchurch in the west to Waterside in the east, from the coast in the south, almost to Salisbury in the north. Currently some 28 per cent of the Forest land is privately owned, 23 per cent is used for growing timber and the remaining 49 per cent is what is known as open forest. The sheer size of the area made it a useful military asset and, indeed, the Forest has been used by the Army for many years, certainly as far back as the First World War.

But, unlike the First War when the civilian population remained relatively unaffected, the impact on the Home Front during the Second World War was to be quite dramatic.

❖ ❖ ❖

Richard Taylor, who now lives in Brockenhurst, used to take holidays in the New Forest. These reminiscences are based on the diary he kept as a boy:

At 11 a.m. on 3 September 1939 British listeners tuned into the BBC, to hear an announcement to stand by for a speech by the Prime Minister, Neville Chamberlain. At 11.15 a.m., he came on the air, his voice tired and strained. Britain had called for an undertaking from Hitler to withdraw German troops from Poland, which had been invaded on 1 September.

'I have to tell you now that no such undertaking has been received,' the Prime Minister said, 'and that consequently this country is at war with Germany.'

When the Prime Minister broadcast, I, aged twelve, was with my sister, fourteen, and brother, sixteen, in a caravan by Wotton Bridge, in the New Forest, which my mother had hired for a fortnight's holiday. We were all, even at that age, very much aware that war was likely to break out. And it showed, really, even in a small family like that how people differed in their approach. Possibly according to their age.

My brother, who was always something of a pessimist, said that he thought that most of us would be dead by Christmas, because the Germans would use poisoned gas and in any case, even if we weren't killed by poison gas, we would all be bombed.

My sister and I were that bit younger and didn't really think that could, or would, happen, at all. What we were concentrating on at the time was going out to the shops to see what sugar and other items we could get, in case there was going to be severe rationing.

But it was a memorable time, and in a very beautiful and quiet part of the New Forest. Members of the family had seen otters, which I never saw, but they were supposed to be in the stream by Wotton Bridge.

Anyway, that was my main memory, but I do remember the very dull, monotonous voice of Neville Chamberlain, saying something extremely important, which even we could understand. Then followed the announcement of the Prime Minister, and a period known as the phoney war in which Brockenhurst experienced the first effects of petrol rationing, and saw the first homesick and disorientated evacuee children arrive on the railway station. The radio, which brought the news of the declaration of war, became a national lifeline. Petrol shortages and blacked-out streets meant that we spent a lot of evenings at home, and few people missed the 9 o'clock news on the BBC Home Service. Through those broadcasts, and the door-by-door delivery of leaflets, we learnt how to secure our homes against air raids. We learnt how to find and use the best food bargains, and how to cook them into a nourishing meal. And how to put up Anderson shelters in our back gardens.

Soon, however, that same radio was to carry news of different import. The phoney war of preparation, and little else, came to an end, and we as a nation began to expect, as first Denmark, then Norway, the Low Countries and France fell, a new wave of Nazi onslaughts. We quickly understood the term Blitzkrieg, or Lightning War – and that war was about to reach Britain's shores and invade every homestead in our country.

Territorial army camps were held in the New Forest each year, but in 1939 these were on a much larger scale than usual, and 30,000 men were to camp at Burley, Beaulieu and East Boldre during August. The local paper said that Lymington was invaded by the Army, with scenes reminiscent of 1914. Indeed, both in times of peace and war the Forest had been used as a military training area.

Major the Right Honourable Anthony Eden took time off from his official duties in mid-August to join his regiment, the 2nd Battalion The Rangers KRRC at East Boldre, near Beaulieu, for a fortnight's training. His 600 troops travelled from Waterloo to Brockenhurst in two special trains, and were then taken by lorry as

A large multi-person air-raid shelter. *(Author's collection)*

Registration of evacuees assisted by the Salvation Army. *(Salvation Army)*

far as Hatchet Pond, just a few miles away and now a favourite beauty spot for tourists. The troops were met by a military band.

On Monday 13 August some Territorial Army soldiers returning by road to London from Beaulieu had an alarming experience when their motorbus failed to clear the very low railway arch at Balmer Lawn, Brockenhurst. The roof of the bus was ripped off from end to end. Fortunately, there were no serious casualties. An NCO at the rear of the bus shouted to the men to dive on to the floor. Amazingly, they all proceeded to London in the remains of the bus, accompanied by a police convoy.

August 1939 was very wet, and the Territorial Army camp, situated on flat, low-lying land at East Boldre, was affected by floods on more than one occasion. Some 7,000 men were washed out of their camp on 3 August and were subsequently billeted in farm buildings and schools throughout the area, in Lymington, Beaulieu, Brockenhurst, Boldre and East Boldre.

Meanwhile, civil defence matters were in hand, with appeals in January for ARP volunteers, including dispatch riders and boy runners, aged sixteen to seventeen. In March a meeting was held at Lymington to explain the complications of ARP administration to the public. Hampshire was effectively divided into seven areas, plus the county boroughs. Area number seven comprised the Borough of Lymington, the New Forest Rural District, and Ringwood and Fordingbridge Rural District. This was in the charge of a salaried assistant county ARP controller, Colonel Daniels, and there was another paid officer, Captain Jarvis. All other workers were volunteers. It was stated that 65 per cent of the ARP service was paid for by the Treasury, the balance coming from the county rates.

ARP exercises and training sessions took place all through the spring and summer, disclosing, as might have been expected, many serious failures of management and communication. There was a mock air raid on Lymington in June, and a trial black-out of the whole of southern England late on the evening of 9 August and early in the morning of 10 August. Even in May local papers were reticent about reporting the huge influx of troops into the area. In any case, the reporters themselves may not have been fully aware of the extent of the build-up. We now know that vast numbers of men and quantities of equipment were skilfully hidden in and around the Forest. The locals, of course, realised that 'something was up': for instance, some roads were being widened, and concrete laid down to take the tanks and heavy military equipment.

During the war, at Brockenhurst, the unusually large village railway station was in constant use day and night as troops and equipment arrived by the trainload. Brockenhurst was an ideal central dispersal point with easy access to the military encampments that were being constructed right across the area. Holmsley station, now a popular tea-room and tourist centre, was also one of the main dispersal points for incoming troops and equipment. Every village and town across the Forest contributed to, and was affected by, the war effort.

Today Brockenhurst is popular with visitors from around the world, many of whom use the village as a base for exploring the Forest. The thousands of visitors have replaced thousands of troops; cars and people carriers have replaced military vehicles; and peace has replaced uncertainty.

❖   ❖   ❖

After the early days of the so-called Phoney War many parts of the country were subjected to enemy bombing and many airfields were targeted as part of the great plan to annihilate our air defence. Later, the whole population held its breath during the evacuation of Dunkirk and the subsequent Battle of Britain.

But more optimistic days were to come. The assault on Fortress Europe, in June 1944, was the culmination of considerable secret planning. The tangible evidence of this great campaign is probably most obvious in the county of Hampshire and specifically within the vast heathlands and woodlands of the New Forest.

Another delivery of stores arrives at a forest camp. *(Hampshire Fire & Rescue Service)*

Churchill tanks arrive in the New Forest. *(Tank Museum)*

It was here, in the New Forest, that a vast army lived, trained and assembled for the D-Day landings. It is here that men and women in their thousands were stationed on the hastily created Advanced Landing Grounds, airfields and naval installations. And here, too, were ordinary civilians whose lives were turned upside down by the invasion of so many British and Allied personnel.

The need to hide armies, the need to have fighter and bomber bases as near to the front line as possible and the need to carry out intelligence and training activities were all served by the ideal terrain and natural landscape within the bounds of the Forest. This huge, complex exercise was not without its problems, however. A complete new infrastructure was needed to cope with the increase in population and the substantial increase in traffic. A road-widening and building programme began in earnest after the decision was taken to use the Forest as a prime preparation area for the D-Day campaign. Photographs taken at the time show contractors widening key access roads on the perimeter of the Forest. At several strategic sites, including one at Totton, access road systems were prepared for the influx of thousands of troops and vehicles.

Evidence of the road-widening programme carried out during the build-up to D-Day is still visible in many parts of the Forest today, particularly in the villages of Pilley near Lymington and Langley and Blackfield, near the embarkation point at Lepe. It is said that the urgency of the entire operation was such that there was no time for consultation with the local community. Records held at the Verderers' Office in Lyndhurst show that workmen moved into an area, widened the road and in the process often removed parts of front gardens, telegraph poles and pavements without any prior warning! Nearly 25 miles of road were widened by an average of 4 feet, which effectively removed 25 acres of Forest land from general use.

The Deputy County Surveyor informed the Verderers that, 'for military purposes, road-widening had been made on some of the minor and district roads through the Forest'. The clerk had written to the County Surveyor asking for an explanation, as no previous notice had been given.

In the early days the planning teams encountered problems with the amounts of compensation offered to commoners for their land, and for the loss of grazing rights on land, which was requisitioned for the building of military installations. Initially, the War Department offered 2s per acre for land requisitioned at Beaulieu and Holmsley South. Over a period of some months negotiations took place and the sum of 4s per acre was finally agreed for land deals at Stoney Cross. Later, this offer was reduced to 2s 6d because the Air Ministry decided that commoners were not entitled to compensation under the Defence Act 1939.

Another convoy arrives. (*Hampshire Fire & Rescue Service*)

(Wessex Film and Sound Archives)

The construction programme under way, early 1940s: road-widening (left) and on the airfield (above). *Below:* A military map identifying training areas in the New Forest.

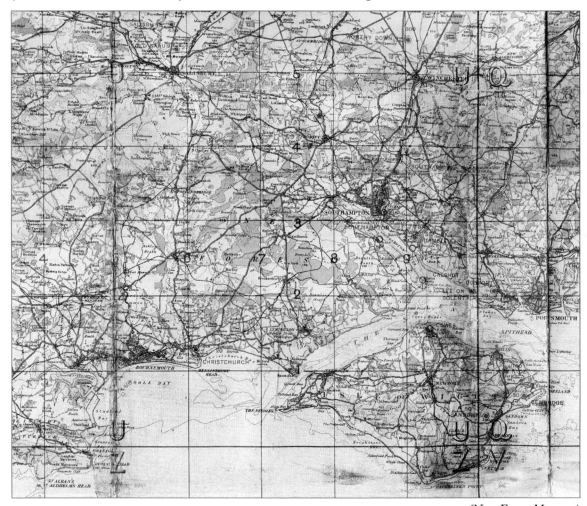

(New Forest Museum)

Further hold-ups in settling claims, however, proved frustrating on both sides, since delay could jeopardise deadlines and broken deadlines would mean the great assault on Europe might have to be postponed. Legal action was mooted when the Air Ministry subsequently withdrew the agreement. And so day-to-day life, with all its problems, went on.

Peter Sadler was staying in the country near New Milton and recalls that enemy aircraft flew over the town.

> I had been evacuated to relatives in the area. It seems we saw more aircraft than my parents did over London. One day I saw a small enemy plane fly over the town. Most of us kids knew what enemy aircraft looked like. It dropped down quite low and I heard the echo of a sort of crack, crack, crack sound. I did not know that it was gunfire at the time, but later it was reported that civilians in the town had been shot at.

Needs Ore Point, south of Beaulieu, was a small Advanced Landing Ground accommodating over 100 Hawker Typhoons. It was occupied in April 1944, but such was the rapid pace of the war that by July 1944 the site had been abandoned! Once the home of a famous wing of the 2nd Tactical Air Force, Needs Ore Point recorded the largest number of sorties reached in one day from any airfield. On this former airfield site the remains of some of the Summerfeld tracking (used as a take-off and landing mat on the grass runways) can be seen today at the entrance to Park Farm. In one of the private gardens on the estate, cables originally used by 356 HAA Battery Royal Artillery for on-site communications are buried just a few inches under the ground. Park Farmhouse was one of many buildings used by the military to support airfield activities.

The stretch of private beach at Needs Ore is littered with brickwork and concrete from the various emplacements and the myriad smaller constructions which once dominated the shoreline. Debris from the heavily camouflaged AA gun sites can also be found. From the air, as with most of the Forest airfields and installations, imprints left as a result of previous usage can be clearly seen.

The majority of the workforce on many of the major construction contracts came from Ireland. At the time Ireland had a vast pool of manpower to call upon and many thousands of men were employed in the building industry, from airfield runways and roads to POW camps and other military installations throughout the region. Indeed, at the height of the building programme as many as 20,000 men were employed on the airfield construction programme alone. A rare image, captured by Sgt O'Neill of the Army Film Unit, shows a British Army engineer using a Caterpillar bulldozer to clear a Forest site ahead of building. Bulldozers and many other types of equipment were flown in from the United States as part of the Lend-Lease Programme.

Many of today's well-known national construction companies, including Wimpey and Laings, were contracted to build the major airfields at Beaulieu, Holmsley South, Stoney Cross, Hurn and Christchurch.

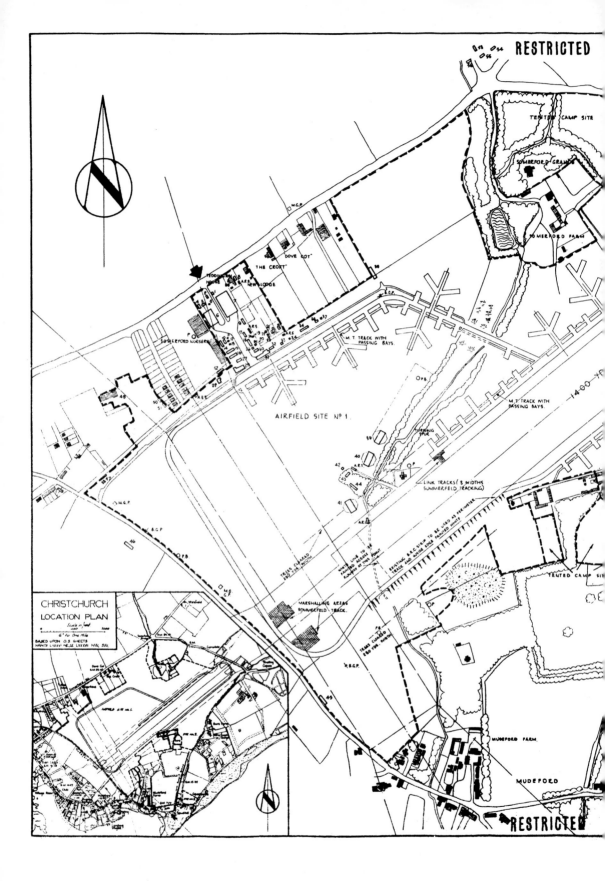

TENTED CAMP SITE

SOMERFORD GRANGE

SOMERFORD FARM

DOVE COT"

THE CROFT"

TEDDINGTON
HOUSE
NEW LODGE

SOMERFORD NURSERY

M.T. TRACK WITH
PASSING BAYS.

AIRFIELD SITE No 1.

M.T. TRACK WITH
PASSING BAYS.

1400 YDS

TURNING
SPUR

LINK TRACKS (3 WIDTHS
SUMMERFELD TRACKING)

EXISTING B.R.C. STRIP TO BE USED AS PERIMETER
TRACK ALSO WHERE SHOWN FORMED TRACK

TRACK CLOSED
380 YDS WIDTH

TENTED CAMP SITE

MARSHALLING AREAS
SUMMERFELD TRACK.

TRACK CLOSED
380 YDS. WIDTH

MUDEFORD FARM

MUDEFORD

CHRISTCHURCH
LOCATION PLAN

Scale in feet

6" to One Mile
BASED UPON O.S. SHEETS
HANTS LXXVI NE.SE LXXXVII NW. SW.

AIRFIELD SITE No I.

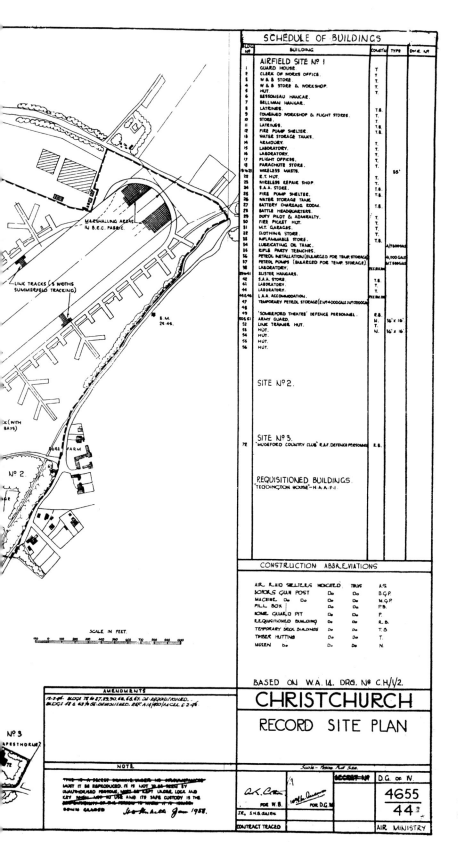

SCHEDULE OF BUILDINGS

BLDG. N°	BUILDING	CONSTN	TYPE	DWG. N°
	AIRFIELD SITE N° 1			
1	GUARD HOUSE	T		
2	CLERK OF WORKS OFFICE	T		
3	W. & B. STORE	T		
4	W. & B. STORE & WORKSHOP	T		
5	HUT	T		
6	BESSONEAU HANGAR			
7	BELLMAN HANGAR			
8	LATRINES	T.B.		
9	COMBINED WORKSHOP & FLIGHT STORES	T		
10	STORE	T		
11	LATRINES	T.B.		
12	FIRE PUMP SHELTER	T.B.		
13	WATER STORAGE TANK			
14	ARMOURY	T		
15	LABORATORY	T		
16	LABORATORY	T		
17	FLIGHT OFFICES	T		
18	PARACHUTE STORE	T		
19 to 21	WIRELESS MASTS		55'	
22	R.T. HUT	T		
23	WIRELESS REPAIR SHOP	T		
24	S.A.A. STORE	T.B.		
25	FIRE PUMP SHELTER	T.B.		
26	WATER STORAGE TANK			
27	BATTERY CHARGING ROOM	T.B.		
28	BATTLE HEADQUARTERS			
29	DUTY PILOT & ADMIRALTY	T		
30	FIRE PICKET HUT	T		
31	M.T. GARAGES	T		
32	CLOTHING STORE	T		
33	INFLAMMABLE STORE	T.B.		
34	LUBRICATING OIL TANK		A/7600GALS	
35	RIFLE PARTY TRENCHES			
36	PETROL INSTALLATION (ENLARGED FOR TEMP. STORAGE)		14,000 GALS	
37	PETROL PUMPS (ENLARGED FOR TEMP. STORAGE)		M.T. 500GALS	
38	LABORATORY	PET. BLK.300		
39 to 41	BLISTER HANGARS			
42	S.A.A. STORE	T.B.		
43	LABORATORY	T		
44	LABORATORY	T		
45&46	L.A.A. ACCOMMODATION	PET. BLK.300		
47	TEMPORARY PETROL STORAGE (2 N° 4000GALS IN N° 12000GAL)			
48				
49	'SOMERFORD THEATRE' DEFENCE PERSONNEL	R.B.		
50 & 51	ARMY GUARD	N.	36' x 16'	
52	LINK TRAINER HUT	T		
53	HUT	N.	36' x 16'	
54	HUT			
55	HUT			
56	HUT			
	SITE N° 2			
	SITE N° 3			
72	'MUDEFORD COUNTRY CLUB' R.A.F. DEFENCE PERSONNEL	R.B.		
	REQUISITIONED BUILDINGS			
	TEDDINGTON HOUSE - N.A.A.F.I.			

CONSTRUCTION ABBREVIATIONS

AIR RAID SHELTERS INDICATED	THUS		A.S.
BOFORS GUN POST	Do	Do	B.G.P.
MACHINE Do Do	Do	Do	M.G.P.
PILL BOX	Do	Do	P.
HOME GUARD PIT	Do	Do	
REQUISITIONED BUILDING	Do	Do	R.B.
TEMPORARY BRICK BUILDINGS	Do	Do	T.B.
TIMBER HUTTING	Do	Do	T.
NISSEN Do	Do	Do	N.

BASED ON W.A.14. DRG. N° C.H./1/2.

CHRISTCHURCH
RECORD SITE PLAN

SCALE IN FEET

AMENDMENTS

BLDGS. 72 to 27, 53, 30, 68, 66, 67. DE-REQUISITIONED. BLDGS. 18 & 63 to 66 DEMOLISHED. REF. A.14/80/16.CELL. 5-2-76.

NOTE

Scale ~ 1/2500 Full Size.

			RECORD N°	D.G. of W.
				4655
FOR W.B.	FOR D.G.W.			**44½**
I.E., S.H.B. GAIRN				
CONTRACT TRACED				AIR MINISTRY

Jan. 1958.

Christchurch airfield site plan.
(Author's collection)

Evacuees give a nervous smile for the camera. *(Salvation Army)*

Just as the military authorities were diligently discharging their obligations under wartime conditions, so too the civilian authorities were engaged in dealing with an increasing workload with a remit that included the fire services, Air Raid Precaution and First Aid. From its offices in Lyndhurst, New Forest Rural District Council was also responsible for taking evacuees from a number of neighbouring towns, including Southampton and Portsmouth. In the early days of evacuation preparations were made for the reception and accommodation of a total of 5,814 evacuees. However, when this first evacuation exercise was carried out on 1 and 2 September 1939 only 2,300 placements were in fact filled.

Southampton evacuated on the Friday and the Saturday with the first groups of children being required to attend the assembly points at 6 a.m. Until noon on these two days the eligible groups of schoolchildren, teachers, registered helpers, toddlers under five years of age and expectant mothers gathered as instructed and were then bussed or sent by train to their allotted destinations.

Local newspapers gave full details of the evacuation programme and whole teams of volunteers and personnel from organisations such as the Salvation Army were pressed into action. The advice to those not being evacuated was to stay away. The railway stations and departure points had to be kept clear of all non-essential travellers. Each evacuee was required to carry provisions for the journey and more besides. The list included knife, fork, spoon, comb, handkerchief, plate, mug and toothbrush, shoes or plimsolls, socks, a change of clothes and of course a gas mask. In total over three million children across the country were evacuated.

Roused from their beds at a very early hour, and still very sleepy, they were suddenly thrust into a completely different life from what they had known before. Many would remain away from home for a long time; many would return as orphans; others would become ill and homesick, which led to ongoing problems in later life. Most adapted as best they could and for some it was a great adventure, despite not having mum around. Although some evacuees were taken in by families just a few miles into the Forest and perhaps no more than forty-five minutes' drive

Some evacuees were taken by bus to their destinations. *(Salvation Army)*

De-lousing was a necessary evil. *(Salvation Army)*

from Southampton, the upheaval, however limited, took all their reserves to cope with. They were traumatic times for everyone involved and it was reported at the time that 'it was impossible to remain unmoved as childish footsteps echoed along the road on this gloomy September morning'.

Local people who opened up their homes to the evacuees were paid the sum of 10*s* 6*d* per week, although this was reduced to 8*s* 6*d* per child for two or more children billeted at the same address.

Accommodation of a more macabre nature was also being arranged. The perceived need for the mass burial of local victims of the war prompted a survey of spaces for graves. It was believed that there would be huge numbers of casualties as a result of poison gas attacks and bombing campaigns against the civilian population. It was reported that there were 7,800 spaces available in cemeteries throughout the district. Subject to certain agreed rules and regulations, ten churches in the area were prepared to permit the use of their buildings as temporary mortuaries. Fortunately, as it turned out, the burial of civilians *en masse* was not something the local authorities would have to deal with.

In excess of 10,000 gas masks were issued immediately to the people of the Forest. Eventually, every man, woman and child was carrying the standard gas mask, in the little brown cardboard box that came to symbolise much of what wartime life was all about. Nationally, a total of 38 million gas masks were issued.

In accordance with public statute, the ringing of church bells was reserved for a call to arms in the event of invasion, so that the many bells, which had previously rung out across the Forest of a Sunday morning, fell silent. They were to ring again several years later at the time of victory in Europe.

Road signs across the Forest were removed. Local people of course knew their way around. Visitors and holidaymakers, however, of which there were still quite a few, experienced some difficulty navigating their way around the Forest and anyone who asked the way was regarded with suspicion: after all, the population was constantly being reminded to stay alert in case of infiltration by enemy spies.

People throughout the country were learning how to use stirrup pumps and how to deal with incendiary bombs, and training in basic ARP skills was extended to many communities. Mock exercises often had the participants in fits of laughter as well as making them recognise that in reality much of what they were being taught would never work in practice.

Writing to his sister after the war, Bob Dowling from Fordingbridge said:

What we learned was a farce. It was all acting. They used a civilian car as a German tank. We had to use tin cans full of gravel as make believe hand grenades. We had to run out alongside the car and throw our cans on the roof. The chances are that a real tank crew would have machine gunned us or done us some other damage before we had a chance to throw grenades. At the time, of course, it all seemed a rather serious business and the people training us did so with all good intent and in the spirit which prevailed at the time.

On the home front the population was taking each day as it came. New rules and regulations affected everything from transport and food to clothing and personal liberty. Everything was labelled 'Utility'. What remains of Utility clothing is now sought after by collectors for its simple style and make-do manufacture. As the Allied Forces began to invade the Forest, food rationing was supplemented by gifts from the servicemen. Candy bars and chocolate were widely and regularly distributed, as were other foodstuffs depending on where in the Forest one lived. Generally speaking, the nearer an American base, the better fed you were. The PXs (the American version of our NAAFI) were stocked to feed at least two armies, so there was always a surplus and the Americans were quite generous.

Margaret Scott, who lived close to Holmsley, recalls:

We got stuff that we would otherwise try and get on the black market. What they call candy we had plenty of and things for some of the girls. Stockings, I mean, and occasionally silk petticoats too. We never went short, but we weren't greedy either. Sometimes people with chickens or allotments would trade with the Americans. Living in the country we were OK and better off than many townsfolk.

In contrast, the diary of Ethel Reid from Lyndhurst records that:

Locally we have a Salvage Drive. I suppose it's happening everywhere. We are taking all sorts down to the collection place. Pots, pans, old books. I gave some of my mother's cutlery that has seen better days. We also have a collection of what's known as pig and bone. Left over foodstuffs really, which is quite funny when you consider we don't have enough to eat anyway.

The Allies – particularly the Americans – found it hard to come to terms with the meagre rations upon which we were supposed to survive. A display at the Totton and Eling Heritage Centre shows the weekly portion of basic foodstuffs such as sugar, eggs and milk. For those with a few shillings in their pocket there was the

Into the unknown, a smiling GI, one of the thousands who were in England for D-Day. *(Courtesy PC, America)*

Under canvas – a welcome break.
(Forestry Commission)

chance to eat out at one of the Forest's many tea-rooms and restaurants. A typical wartime menu offered a roast lunch, a pudding (usually a traditional apple pie) and a cup of coffee, all for the princely sum of 2*s* 6*d*. The Americans in particular enjoyed eating out, and the typical English breakfast and afternoon tea became a ritual with many servicemen.

'It is so essentially English. This country seems so civilised. Are they at war because of this?' wrote a GI in the visitors' book at one popular Forest café.

❖   ❖   ❖

As the weeks and months rolled by through 1943 and 1944, so the numbers of service personnel from Britain and the Allied nations increased. Great tented towns were being created under the cover of the thick Forest plantations, and vehicles and military hardware was being stored on roadsides and on the heath and pasturelands.

Meanwhile, in churchyards right across the Forest, including those at Boldre, Bransgore and Brockenhurst, many hundreds of men, aircrew in particular, were laid to rest on an almost day-to-day basis. Although the majority of deaths were a result of combat, sadly quite a number of pilots and crew were killed when their aircraft crashed on take-off or landing. Nevertheless, their deaths were still reported as 'killed in action' and their relatives were notified accordingly. The close proximity of each of the new airfields to each other meant that collisions were inevitable and in the early days of the establishment of the Forest airfields crash crews were kept quite busy.★

Before and during the build-up to D-Day some areas in the Forest were designated for training purposes for everything from small arms to tanks, espionage to bombing. Acres of land were requisitioned for the purpose. Each area was ideally suited to the specific

On exercise, Pylewell, *c.* 1942. *(Lord Teynham)*

★ It is reported that sometimes such was the damage to the crashed aeroplane that it was simply bulldozed into a large hole excavated on the perimeter of the airfield.

Tank training range, New Forest, *c*. 1941. *(Tank Museum)*

needs of the various training units – a tour of the Forest will reveal just how diverse the landscape is, with hillocks and valleys, woods and wide open spaces, streams, lakes and heathland.

Today on former small arms training sites, including the area around Whitemoor Plain, situated mainly in the southern sector, it is still possible to recover spent bullets and mortar rounds. Thousands of live rounds were fired and discarded as training intensified. Remains of field telephone installations can also be seen.

The training of tank crews in the Forest seemed a more sensitive issue than exploding bombs. The Official Verderer refers to an emergency meeting with Major Partridge and a major from the Guards Armoured Division regarding an urgent request to exercise tanks in the Burley Pastures and the Beaulieu Pastures. The two areas were agreed upon, and to keep in constant touch with the Agister* and to give advance notice of intended exercises three mounted men were employed to follow the tanks.

---

* Agister: person responsible for animals in the New Forest.

As we now know, of course, the area eventually became one huge military community, with RAF, Naval and Army establishments operating almost side by side. In all an area of some 20,000 acres was requisitioned for war purposes. The cost in compensation and construction was colossal. Ashley Number 9 Range alone is recorded in local government papers as having cost £80,000, the equivalent today of about £8,000,000.

The bombing ranges at Ashley, near Godshill, on the road between Cadnam and Fordingbridge, were on active service twenty-four hours a day. A few relics of the site are still in evidence today, although only the most intrepid will discover those hidden deep in the undergrowth. However, a huge concrete slab, which was used as part of the targeting system, has only recently been removed from the highest point on the site. Its imprint is still clearly visible from ground level and map-readers will notice reference to it on Ordnance Survey sheets of the area. The aptly named Snake Road effectively splits the ranges in two. Originally used as a service road, it is now popular with walkers and riders. Ashley Ranges

Snake Road, Ashley Ranges, as seen from the road to Godshill. *(Author's collection)*

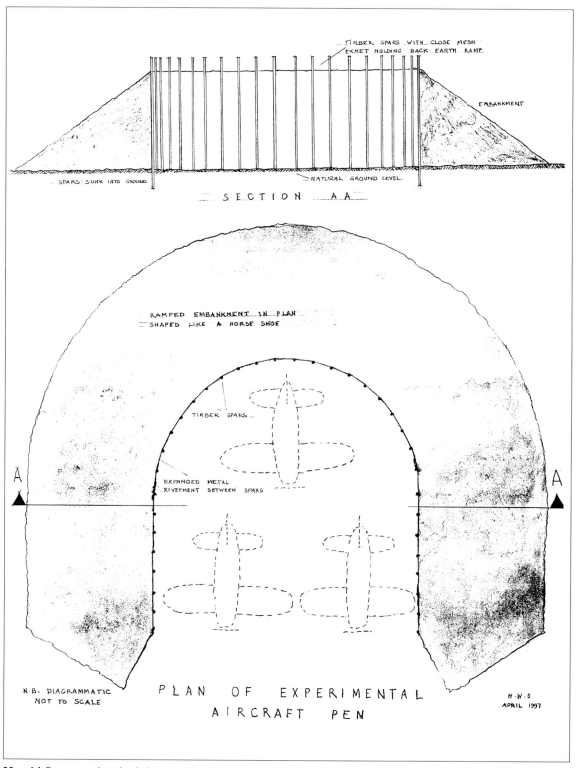

TIMBER SPARS WITH CLOSE MESH
EXMET HOLDING BACK EARTH RAMP.

EMBANKMENT

SPARS SUNK INTO GROUND

NATURAL GROUND LEVEL.

SECTION AA

RAMPED EMBANKMENT IN PLAN
SHAPED LIKE A HORSE SHOE

TIMBER SPARS

EXPANDED METAL
RIVETMENT BETWEEN SPARS

A

A

N.B. DIAGRAMMATIC
NOT TO SCALE

PLAN OF EXPERIMENTAL
AIRCRAFT PEN

H.W.S
APRIL 1997

Harold Sturgess sketched the pens he helped to build. *(Author's collection)* were used as one of the test sites for the Barnes-Wallis bouncing bomb and were subsequently used to test other new bombs and bombing techniques.

Further along the road, near the Fighting Cocks public house, is a gravel track, which leads to another section of the Ashley site. It is here that Harold Sturgess, as one of a team of engineers, was responsible for building open dummy aircraft pens in December 1943 and January 1944, on what is known as Godshill Ridge. He explains:

> We built several of what were called experimental aircraft pens. Five or six, I can't be sure. Earth banks were built up and reinforced with corrugated sheeting. Stakes were driven into the ground to hold the sheeting in place. They were quite big constructions but I can't remember now exactly the height and size. Later we took a delivery of some very old pre-war aeroplanes. Again, I can't remember what they were, biplanes of some type I think. They were placed into the pens.
>
> Some days later, some aircraft came over the site and started to strafe and bomb the pens. We thought it was normal training, but later discovered it was all part of the build-up to D-Day.
>
> I remember when the old aircraft arrived on Queen Mary trailers. They were parked up for some time until we were ready to load them into the pens. Several of the lads, myself included, removed lots of the instruments and interesting bits. They would be worth a fortune now if only I had kept them.

Elsewhere in the Forest, less important matters had to be dealt with. A particular cause for concern among the Forest elders was that of traffic violations. It had been reported how military vehicles were speeding through the narrow Forest lanes causing danger to animals and pedestrians alike. On camps around the Forest the speed limit was just 5 mph, but there are no records to confirm the maximum speed on the highway! Anyway, the Army had a tendency to ignore laws that applied to the civilian population, having its own rules and regulations, and driving vehicles at speed was not, in the great scheme of things, of much concern to them. Nevertheless, they issued a note asking drivers to co-operate with the request. The whole matter passed very quickly into memory and vehicles continued to be driven at whatever speed suited the driver!

A GMC truck of the type seen by the hundred in the New Forest.
(Author's collection)

2
Recollections of D-Day

By 1943 the terrible Allied shipping losses began to reduce as the U-boat war subsided in the face of stiffened Allied resolve and greater resources. The Americans had committed their armies, and supplies of both men and equipment tipped the balance in favour of Britain. Britain was now a huge floating military installation with close on one and a half million Allied servicemen and women crammed into this tiny island.

As a young lad Jimmy Charlton watched the arrival of American troops in Brockenhurst:

> The girls were waving and cheering. Most people were smiling. The soldiers all seemed to be very well built and they were loaded down with equipment and guns. Most were either smoking or chewing gum. I think everyone was pleased to see them. Later, they arranged games and parties for the children. There were dances to which everyone went and had a great time.

And so the great build-up to Operation Overlord (D-Day) was under way and continued apace for many months. Many of the men who were to assemble along the south coast for the operation had been assigned to their camps in the New Forest. Training featured large in the life of troops stationed in and around the Forest where ranges and assault courses proliferated. Beach landings were practised at various sites along the Forest coastline.

As men and machines swamped the Forest, American and British troops increased security. Many of the camps were self-contained, with their own, albeit makeshift, facilities and services, including cinemas, hospitals and canteens. Daily briefings and exercises kept the troops alert and ready for the action ahead. An Army marches on its stomach, so they say, and mealtimes were always a welcome diversion from the strict routines of the day. Other welcome diversions included improvised games and the chance to write a letter home and to meet the neighbours!

Archive footage still exists of commandos being briefed by Lord Lovat in a clearing somewhere deep in the Forest: hundreds of men, unaware of what lies ahead of them, unaware that they are about to change the course of world history. We will never know how many survived and how many paid the supreme

The Northumberland Fusiliers undergo infantry training at Pylewell. *(Lord Teynham)*

A convoy of fire appliances with dispatch riders on exercise. *(Hampshire Fire & Rescue Service)*

sacrifice. We can only think about them as they prepared for battle, guess at their hopes, their fears and their aspirations. Ordinary men plunged into an extraordinary situation. The next door neighbour, the friend, the brother, the father, the lover.

And just as there were many foot soldiers, so too there were mechanised divisions. Day after day, hundreds of tanks and heavy equipment took up position in the lanes and on the streets throughout the Forest. Convoys of vehicles alerted the population to the fact that 'something big' was about to happen.

❖   ❖   ❖

Dr Basil Fulton, who practised in Lymington and Brockenhurst, shares his thoughts on life in the area at the time of D-Day:

Things began to liven up when they started to widen country lanes and put in hard standings. One-way systems were created, which made it very difficult for me to get around, and I did not have the petrol for lengthy detours.

I found that if a route was not guarded by a 'Snowdrop' (an American military policeman) there was a fair chance that there would be no oncoming traffic, and I could nip through the wrong way and get away with it.

Along the verge of Sway Road, in Brockenhurst, they had lines of vehicles being made amphibious by the application of a kind of soft, sticky, silicone grease good for plumbing repairs, if you could get at it.

About a week before D-Day all personnel were gathered in briefing camps, hidden all over the Forest. They were briefed on their coming tasks and objectives and how they were expected to carry them out.

There was a camp across the Beaulieu to Lyndhurst road, and as I would have had a long detour I insisted on being allowed to drive through, which I was. But with a sentry on my running board, his rifle at my ear, and directions not to look right or left, but keep my eyes on the road.

In the briefing camps all personnel were arranged into groups, with their vehicles and equipment ready for embarkation. We had one soldier in the theatre at Lymington Hospital, with appendicitis, at this time; he had an armed guard to ensure that he said nothing.

To illustrate how difficult it was to get around the area in those days, I had a confinement at a farm, a bit beyond Sowley on the coast, Lepe way, and set off over the level crossing, through the toll bridge, signed the book at the causeway control point, giving a reason for the journey. Went past Elmers Court, Lymington, opened and closed the gates on either side of the runway at Pylewell Aerodrome, which ran across the road. Then through the forest gates at Broomhill, and through another runway with gates by St Leonards Grange. Needless to say I was too late for the birth of a baby girl, who, by the way, I still meet occasionally.

Of course there were few civilian doctors about and life was very hectic. A

Elmers Court, Lymington, was requisitioned for the war effort. *(Author's collection)*

day could start with anaesthetics at Lymington Hospital followed by surgeries at Lymington or Brockenhurst. A round of visits in East Boldre, afternoon surgery in Sway, which was in the front room of a private house, and visits or more surgeries in the evening. With all this moving around, I was perhaps uniquely placed to see the build-up to D-Day and its effect on the area.

On D-Day minus one, I was visited by a patient at a cottage on the shore by Pitts Deep and had the impression of being able to walk right across to the Island from craft to craft, the Solent being so full of them.

I slept through the exodus, having been very busy the preceding days. The enormous air armada that passed over at low level to avoid enemy radar left me quite undisturbed. But everyone was talking about it the following day. In the next day or so as I was walking down Belmore Road one warm, sultry evening I could hear the gunfire from the Normandy beachhead.

❖   ❖   ❖

In the first few crucial days of June 1944 embarkation began at ports and jetties all along the south coast. The waters off the Forest coastline were packed full of boats. Men and machines were loaded day and night on to the many assembled boats. These included landing craft and Minka barges, constructed locally. Mulberry Harbours, built on the Beaulieu river and at Lepe, were ready for towing out to the invasion beaches.

On the twelve airfields contained within the Forest boundary, squadrons were kept at various states of readiness. 'Released' meant that the squadron was not required to operate until a specified hour and the personnel could be employed elsewhere on other duties. 'Available' meant that the squadron had to be prepared to be in the air within so many minutes of receiving the order.

'Readiness' was recognised as the most advanced state. Occasionally, however, the 'Stand-by' state was used, which meant that the pilots were seated in their aircraft with the engines off, but with the aircraft pointing into the wind ready to start up and take off the moment the leader got orders from the station controller.

As we know, the invasion, originally scheduled for launch on 5 June, was postponed for twenty-four hours. During this time the troops were confined to the boats and ships to which they had been allocated. The ration packs they had been issued with were replaced with fresh stocks and eating became an enthusiastic pastime, which helped to relieve the boredom. So too did swotting up on the French language!

June 1944, the month that changed the course of modern world history. Men

Embarkation!
(Wessex Film and Sound Archives)

Ready for the off,
June 1944. *(Wessex Film
and Sound Archives)*

and machines in their thousands began the assault on Fortress Europe. The years of preparation now consolidated into the one day of the push, and the following days of offensive action, which would make or break the war for the Allies. Wave after wave of aircraft left the airfields of the Forest, boats left from every part of the Forest coastline. The build-up had taken months. In contrast, the Forest was empty of men and machines within a matter of hours. There was an eerie silence.

Of the 4,000-plus warships used in support of the landings, many left from the Solent and other moorings along the Forest coastline. On day one, D-Day itself, over 150,000 troops survived the German defensive actions and managed to get ashore and make some advance. Some 2,500 soldiers however, mainly from the American divisions, perished, although this was many fewer than the Army had imagined would be killed on the first day.

Maurice Taylor was an eleven-year-old schoolboy at the time of the invasion and recalls:

We were able to go into some of the deserted Camps that had been on high security only hours before. We were given some food rations. There were some soldiers left behind. When we asked where everybody had gone, one of the soldiers laughed and said, 'they have gone to give Mr Hitler a big surprise'. It was a day later that my parents read the full news of D-Day.

The fire service provided cover for the convoys bound for points of embarkation. *(Hampshire Fire & Rescue Service)*

This was the beginning of the end of the Second World War in Europe. Although peace was a year away, the mood of the country was one of great optimism. Many rules and regulations were relaxed, and although rationing continued life began to improve for everyone.

One by one the airfields of the Forest were put on a care and maintenance basis. A few remained in use for a couple of years after the war, but for the most part they very quickly became redundant. RAF Fighter Command

USAAF pilots at Winkton, 1944. *(John Levesley)*

alone   had   contributed   30,000   aeroplanes
during   the   six   years   of   war.   Many   of   these
had flown from the airfields of the Forest. Of the 70,000 airmen who had
perished, many had left from Beaulieu, Holmsley South, Hurn, Winkton and
Stoney Cross.

The Army had left a huge void right across the Forest. The vast armada of boats
and ships had disappeared from the Solent, the Beaulieu river and from all along
the coastline. Hundreds of buildings stood empty. Where once there had been
frantic activity, there was now complete silence. Today that void is represented by
a handful of sites which still reveal evidence of military occupation. The passer-by
might not be aware of the significance of these sites. Holidaymakers and visitors in
their thousands are able to enjoy the delights of the Forest because of the freedom
won for us by men who were based in, and left from, the Forest.

The announcement of Germany's surrender was greeted with joy by most but
by others with disbelief and nagging doubts. Grace Welling remembers that her
mother was 'overwhelmed with emotion' and for days after the announcement was

'not herself'. The relief was mixed with sadness at the thought of the deaths of so many innocent people and the question, 'Why did it have to happen?'

Joyce Baker, on the other hand, recalls:

The street party and celebrations went on for days, with people donating the food, the drinks, the music and the entertainment. There was a gentleman in our village who was always regarded as a recluse. Even he joined in and he actually turned out to be quite a skilled conjuror. Us kids loved it. It was a marvellous time for us all.

So within a year or so of June 1944 the war in Europe was over; and it was peacetime; but it would never be 'back to normal' for the people of the Forest or elsewhere across the nation. The war changed technology, farming and construction: it changed everything, including attitudes, opinion and to a lesser degree class barriers. Molly Saggers recalls:

When my husband Stan returned from Germany, he was treated like a hero. Promises were made about him still having a job at the mill, but it never happened. Many so-called heroes could not find work when they returned home and it was a sad sight in some of the towns to see men having to sell goods from trays round their necks. A petty employment but because everyone had learned how to ration everything, including the number of people in their workforce, jobs were lost.

Alan Crawford, who remarked that the upper classes and the working class fought side by side during the war, gives a different account:

Many of your toff types saw us differently after that. They knew us to be of the same spirit, fighting for a free Britain and a free world. We taught them a lot and they showed us a trick or two.

As the war in Europe came to an end, people ventured back to the Forest. Watching out for the coastal defences and the litter of military occupation was a great pastime for many of the local and visiting children. Jimmy Charlton remembers:

We had great times out and about on our old bikes, finding all sorts of stuff. We found tinned food, pieces of equipment that to this day I don't know what they were, also helmets and spent ammunition. We kept away from the live ammunition. One lad lost some fingers playing with ammunition so we knew it was silly. But no, it was like a treasure hunt really.

A visitor from London wrote:

We love the Forest. We came before the war as a family. Now only my brother

The dedication of the Ibsley Memorial brought together young and old alike.
(Author's collection)

and I remain. The peace here helps us find a way of dealing with the intolerable
stress of a very long war.

While those displaced by the war gradually returned to their own communities,
others made the decision to stay in or near the Forest. Life in the postwar world
was more peaceful, but still austere with rationing in place and restrictions on many
goods and materials. The black market still existed if you knew where to go and
someone, somewhere, would always find just what you were looking for. For some
the changes ushered in by the war offered a new beginning. Women were, at long
last, held in more esteem than they were in the 1930s. Their vital contribution to
the war effort and the sense of independence gained by those who had served in
the Forces meant that the equality factor had to be taken into consideration.

Ethel Reid remembers that some women were taking work as drivers, having
driven trucks and cars in the Army.

It became more common to see women behind the wheel after the war. Driving
commercial vehicles was always regarded as man's work but some of my friends
for example had driven buses in Southampton when the men were called up and

Women played a vital part in the war effort. *(New Forest Museum)*

they wanted to continue to have their own wages rather than rely on a handout from their husbands.

The late 1940s and early 1950s saw increases in visitor numbers to the Forest and an increase in the population, with many ex-servicemen and women, and some ex-Axis forces prisoners of war, settling in the area. Marriages and divorces reflected the changing society and the legacy of the friendly invasion by so many British and Allied troops. Many new friendships developed between people who had given shelter to evacuees and those who had stayed 'away from home' during the early years of the war. Tom Felton was an evacuee who stayed in Brockenhurst:

After the war we went several times to visit the family who had taken in me and my brother. They moved away and we lost touch but we did hear that the man and women of the house had passed away from illness in the late 1950s. I have taken my grandchildren to the house where we stayed. It brings a tear to my eye to think that we survived the war and went on to have a great family. At the time though we never thought we would make it.

Road-widening took place in many Forest villages during the war, as at Pilley.
(*Author's collection*)

The legacy of those times is still visible today. People still lay flowers all year round at Canada Cross, where the Canadians held services before D-Day. The hard-standings at Lepe Beach, a site for Mulberry Harbour construction and launch, the widened roads at Pilley where the heavy vehicles were laid up before loading, the remaining section of runway at Beaulieu airfield and the water tower at Stoney Cross airfield are all there to help keep the memory alive.

However, the most poignant reminders are the many war graves scattered in cemeteries from Ringwood in the west of the Forest to Fawley on the southern tip at the entrance to Southampton Water. It is worth taking a little time to visit and to think about the stories behind each of the names etched on the headstones. Watch out too for the growing number of plaques and memorial stones erected by many history groups and veterans' associations. The memorials at the former Ibsley airfield are excellent examples.

No one can fail to be impressed by the beauty and uniqueness that is the New Forest; however, during the Second World War the area was absolutely vital to the war effort, given its geographical location and natural resources put to use. In the build-up to and at the launch of D-Day the Forest became an integral and strategic component of the Allied planning and execution of 'the Great Adventure'. There is a contrast between the impact of war in the area and the subsequent development of the tourist industry.

The Forest is regarded as a natural playground, where visitors from across the country and the world enjoy holidays which may include walking, fishing, golf, cycling, sailing and much more. This would not have been possible if the Allies had

3

'Under the command of General Eisenhower, Allied naval forces,
supported by strong air forces, began landing Allied armies this morning
on the coast of France.'

This brief radio announcement came as no surprise to the people of the
New Forest. For several years they had been witness to the steady build-up
of men and machines, which by 1944 virtually swamped the area.

*During the final weeks and days preceding that wireless broadcast at 9.00 a.m. on the
morning of 6 June, there was an 'air of anticipation, excitement, yet foreboding' according
to Les Dean.*

I had served my time with an engineering company involved in war work and
when I saw the columns of vehicles and tanks arriving in and around Ringwood
I wondered if any of them were fitted with parts I had made. I doubt that they were,
but it was a cheering thought. The sheer scale of what was happening is difficult to
describe. Everyone knew this could now be the 'beginning of the end' as Winston
Churchill once said, but I couldn't help feeling very nervous. The men who came
in their thousands all seemed to be very jolly, yet one can only imagine what each
individual was thinking, hoping and praying for. No one individual was really aware
of the scale of what one commentator was to call, the Great Adventure.

*Ron Walsh hailed from Lymington and joined the Royal Navy in 1936. He served for
thirty-three years until his retirement in 1969, although his association with the service
continued until 1984 during which time he was a civilian driver at HMS Collingwood.
The preparations for D-Day remain as clear in his mind as though the events happened a
matter of months rather than decades ago.*

'It was on 15 October 1943 that I was among a draft of fifty ratings that sailed
from Liverpool to Boston, Massachusetts, on board the *Aquitania*. We were to take
over a new warship, one of the many built in America as part of the original Lease
Lend Programme which had been agreed some years previously between Roosevelt
and Churchill. After we disembarked from the *Aquitania* about five days later, we
were entrained almost immediately to USN *Saker*, a navy yard which was to be
our temporary home until such times as our vessel was complete. We were at *Saker*
until 6 December 1943 when HMS *Kingsmill*, our ship, was ready for acceptance
trials. After 'shake down' trials in nearby Casco Bay, we were ready to sail for

Ron Walsh RN.

England. Of all the escorts manned by the Royal Navy, only two were built with a specific pre-planned role. The two vessels were our own and the sister ship HMS *Lawford* and both were designated as Headquarters Ships for the planned invasion of Occupied Europe. The ships would anchor off the British sector of the beaches in Normandy. Of course, none of us knew this at the time.'

Once back in England the ships were upgraded at the Cammell Laird Shipyard in Liverpool. HMS *Kingsmill*, a 'Captain Class' Frigate had been laid down on 9 July and was launched a month later on 13 August. Officially commissioned on 29 October 1943, HMS *Kingsmill* K484 was designated as the HQ Ship for Gold Beach. Many modifications were made, including an extra mast for the array of radio and radar communication aerials and an additional sixteen Oerlikon anti-aircraft guns. In May 1944, HMS *Kingsmill* joined HMS *Lawford* at anchor in the Solent, just off the coastline of the New Forest. There they waited day in, day out, the crew observing the frenetic activity both on the water and on the land in the mid distance. Men, machines, equipment, vessels as far as the eye could see in every direction.

Meanwhile across the Forest, north-west of the Solent at Station 414 the 508th Fighter Bomber Squadron, 404th Fighter Bomber Group of the USAAF recorded in their Historical Diaries for May 1944:

On May 11 1944 this squadron became operational fulfilling the hopes and desires of all its members since activation. The first mission was uneventful, but due to the tension of going into combat for the first time it will be remembered by all members of the squadron as one of our most difficult missions. Fly specks on canopies were 'Bogies', Bogies were undoubtedly 'Bandits'. (Bogie was code for an unidentified aircraft, Bandit was an enemy aircraft.)

All flak, no matter how inaccurate, was always heavy and intense – the highest official categorisation describing flak activity as reported in the mission reports. The briefing was very detailed and lengthy and the interrogation a frenzy of mixed emotions and exuberant tales. Happily enough, when the smoke of battle had cleared we concluded it to be an uneventful fighter sweep. On the same day we had another fighter sweep, this time making a deeper penetration into France and this mission too was uneventful.

Having once broken the ice with our first mission, we were set now to take everything that might come in our stride, but to get into bad weather and back again to the tortuous grind of listening to inteliigence officers in ground school, was a horrible ordeal.

May 7 1944

Good weather again favoured us and the squadron had its first dive-bombing mission. Col. McColpin, our Group Commander, led the mission as well as our first two, due to the fact that Major Moon, our Squadron Commander, was flying with another group to gain some combat experience. We dive-bombed marshalling yards at Arras with very good results.

May 8 1944

Found the boys very excited returning from a fighter sweep. They had seen their first enemy aircraft. Me109s and FW190s were seen between Chalons and Reims but they didn't attack. Major Moon led our squadron for the first time on this mission.

May 9 1944

Found our boys attacking a rocket gun target (*V1 launch site*) direct hits were observed on the target and flak that had everybody holding their breath was encountered at Neufchatel. Again on the 9th, we flew top cover for the 507th squadron which attacked another rocket gun target and this mission was very uneventful.

May 10 1944

Again we were blasting railroads attacking the yards at Arras. Major Moon and Bob Johnson cleared the target area of flak by dropping fragmentation bombs on the target before the remainder of the group attacked. They flew so low they had to turn to avoid colliding with the water tower of the town.

May 11 1944

Found our boys escorting heavies for the first time. It was a gruelling mission of four hours' duration. Joe Sherwood, our Operations Officer, led this mission and upon returning said his seat was worn out and he wanted to know where the hell the Luftwaffe was, after all going to Saarbrucken on a long four-hour mission was long enough for Goering to send up some of his boys and if he had to wear out his seat for four hours Herr Goering should send up some planes to relieve the boredom.

May 13 1944

Again we were top cover while the 506th and 507th squadrons of our group dive-bombed the marshalling yard at Tournai. The mission was uneventful.

May 19 1944

Our target was Beaumont-sur-Oise Aerodrome but weather made it impossible for us to attack. However we had our first encounter with Jerry. Six Me109s jumped our squadron near Rouen which was extremely unfortunate for them. When the shooting was over we had our first victory. Ben Kitchens dived after a 109 from 12,000ft and caught him at 500ft and shot him down. On take-off Jack Connor failed to get his heavily loaded Thunderbolt in the air and crashed at the end of the runway considerably damaging his aircraft. Everyone heaved a sigh of relief when they saw Jack jump out of his ship uninjured. Jack said that this was the time he heard those bells ringing.

May 20 1944

Again we served as escort for B26s attacking Evreux Fauville Aerodrome near Paris mission was uneventful.

May 21 1944

Our mission was to attack rolling stock south-east of Paris but bad weather forced us to return without making an attack.

May 22 1944

Found our boys on what Drexel Morgan called the 'milk run' – as easy as the milkman delivering milk door-to-door. We were ordered to attack Bethune for the third time and our pilots found it great sport to tear up the railway yards again.

May 23 1944

Again we served as guardian angels to B26s attacking targets in the Caen area, mission was uneventful.

May 24 1944

Found us again on what our pilots called the seat-hardener mission. On this occasion we escorted B24s to Paris and returned. Upon interrogation Sam Selkregg shouted with his buoyant enthusiasm 'No Hits, No Runs, No Errors', meaning mission uneventful.

May 25 1944

Our mission was escorting B26s to Liege, Belgium, and again results uneventful.

May 28 1944

Again we escorted B26s to Liege – mission uneventful.

May 29 1944

Our mission was to escort B17s returning from Berlin. Our squadron made its deepest penetration into the continent. Making rendezvous with the bombers at Grebenham was uneventful but bad luck dogged our take-off and landing. Harry Nystrom failed to get his heavily laden ship in the air and crashed on the end of the runway. He luckily escaped without a scratch. Ed Pounds caught some flak in the tail of his ship and his tailwheel failed to lower when he landed. His ship was under control at first but with no tailwheel it became unmanageable and rather than crash into some ships that were taxiing, he jammed on the brakes and his ship nosed over and went on its back. Ed escaped with only a small cut on his head, a very lucky pilot.

May 30 1944

Our mission was to escort heavy bomber stragglers from Holland, mission uneventful.

May 31 1944

Found us again to be supporting heavy bombers but old man weather dogged us and rendezvous was not made. Joe Landa said he heard the bells ringing when he spun from 15,000ft while in the overcast, finally pulling out at 2,000ft, a harrowing experience.

Summarising May we find the squadron flew a total of 22 missions with a breakdown as follows, 3 fighter sweeps, 7 dive-bombing missions, and 12 escort missions. After a month of operations every member of the squadron recognised that our excellent record was due to the tireless work and excellent leadership of Major Leo C. Moon.

We are happy to report we dropped 42½ tons of bombs, successfully escorted B26s, B24s and B17s, destroyed one enemy aircraft and suffered no casualties among our ranks.

Also due much credit for the success of our squadron in May are the enlisted men of our squadron whose tireless efforts enabled us to accomplish our excellent record.

Aircraft from the airfields of the New Forest contributed to the 25,275 sorties flown between 9.00 p.m. on 5 June to 9.00 p.m. on 6 June. An aircraft took off from England approximately every three and a half seconds during both day and night.

❖   ❖   ❖

On 5 June 1944 Ron Walsh recorded that his thoughts were 'mixed and confused'. 'Are we going to be blasted back into the sea by the enemy? Whatever happens it is certain that many among this mighty armada will not return from this venture.'

Meanwhile, in the Signallers' Office situated in the basement of Exbury House, Jean Gadston was responsible for typing up the instructions for the Fleet. 'The establishment by then was sealed and although there was a false start on 5 June, on the morning of the 6th, I passed the instruction to the flotilla in the Solent and in Southampton Water and to the Landing Craft in the Beaulieu River to sail.'

Margery Crowe, one of the many WRENS involved in providing vital 'back room' support, was responsible for typing the invasion orders for Force G, which was landing on Gold Beach. She recalls, 'The King boarded the HQ ship and inspected the invasion flotilla. I had been involved in the planning of the training exercises for the crews and men of the Landing Craft fleet in Weymouth. Then via London and Southampton I arrived at HMS *Mastodon*, based at Exbury House, near Hythe in Hampshire.'

2,727 ships sailed by their own power on D-Day, with some craft of the original armada not sailing on that day. Of the recorded total of 5,333 vessels forming the armada, this figure includes landing craft and smaller vessels carried on many of the larger ships. Reflecting the size of the naval operation, orders for the day were 3 inches thick on foolscap paper.

By 08.30 hours on the morning of 6 June, HMS *Kingsmill** under the command of Lieutenant G.H. Cook, was anchored off Gold Beach. 'It was total chaos,' recalls Ron. 'The noise was deafening, gunfire, rifle fire, shouts, screams, shells exploding. The RAF was continually bombing the area behind the beaches. By the dawn of D-Day +1 it was known that our troops had done well ashore and a foothold had

Ron Walsh today.

been established. A party of ratings was able to go ashore after about five days when the activities became more settled.'

As events unfolded on the landing grounds of Northern France, King George VI broadcast to the nation, 'If from every place of worship, from home and factory, from men and women of all ages and many races and occupations, our supplication rise, then, please God, both now and in a future not remote, the predictions of an ancient psalm may be fulfilled. The Lord will give strength unto his people, the Lord will give his people the blessing of peace.'

D-Day and H-Hour are standard military expressions with H-Hour referring,

⋆ Battle Honours were awarded to HMS *Kingsmill*, which later took part in the landings on the Dutch island of Walcheren and to HMS *Lawford*.

HMS *Kingsmill* was returned to the United States Navy on 26 January 1946 and was scrapped a year later on 17 February 1947. HMS *Lawford* was sunk off Gold Beach.

Hurst Castle on Keyhaven Spit guarded the western waters of the Solent. *(Steve Trotter, NFNPA)*

during this operation, to the moment of landing, 6.30 a.m., at the western sector of the landing area. 'D-Day' had by the time of the invasion become a common public phrase used to describe the time when all the planning, preparation and build-up translated into action.

not had access to and the opportunity to use one of the country's prime natural resources.

4

RAF Ibsley: Spitfire Days

Off the main Salisbury to Ringwood road, along the western edge of the Forest, there are a number of tiny hamlets. Many of them remain little changed since the 1940s, when even the smallest communities comprising just a farm and a few houses were caught up in the 'war on the home front'.

Military training grounds, camps and later airfields had swamped much of the New Forest and had an impact on its people and its way of life. One such community was Ibsley, where a large airfield (built by various contractors including Gazes of London) formed the core of a much larger complex which included remote sites at Gorley. A substantial command centre was set in the high ground due east of the control tower and scatterings of ancillary buildings were located throughout the immediate vicinity. Today the old control tower is the site of a nature reserve and is a place of pilgrimage for many veterans, families and those interested in the country's wartime history.

❖   ❖   ❖

Dennis Carter was born in Ringwood in 1927. He was twelve years old when war was declared and he has clear memories of that time. Dennis has always lived and worked in the Forest, and now lives at Burley.

I heard about the outbreak of war in much the same way as I suppose everyone else did. It came on the wireless and then word spread very quickly. I suppose it's the bad news that always travels the fastest.

Anyway, I was twelve and in Ringwood and at that age was already in the local Army Cadets. I didn't really take that much notice of what was going on. At Cadets we did all the usual sorts of training and drill and nothing much really changed although later we were allowed to take our .303 rifles home with us. That was at about the time that everyone thought there would be an invasion by the Germans. Later, everything settled down a bit more.

We hadn't had much practice on the rifles, but had learnt to field strip them and put them back together. Goodness knows what would have happened if we had been called upon to use them. It's a frightening thought, but that's the way things were and people seemed to accept the situation.

I was at school locally and some evenings, with some other chaps, I did fire watching on the roof of the local council offices. I think we started about 8 p.m. and went through till maybe the early hours, taking it in turns to sleep and watch, then back home to get some breakfast and off to school.

When I was about fourteen, just turned, I left school, which was the age you did leave in those days, and I went to work in a greengrocers in Ringwood for 10s per week.

A while after that I was approached by a chap who was working on the new Ibsley airfield site. They were building all sorts of military places in the Forest at that time and we thought it was just another part of the war effort. Little did we know it was to contribute to D-Day in 1944.

Anyway, this chap asked me if I was interested in a job at Ibsley, on the labouring side. The money was an amazing £3 per week. I accepted of course and was soon up on site with many hundreds of other contractors who had come from all over the country and from Ireland. My employers were a company called Gazes and I think they were a London firm.

We had a permit to get on to the site, which was guarded by the RAF, probably the police, I am not sure. I was there from about 8 o'clock in the morning till late in the afternoon and we were busy all day long, day in day out. There was a lot of building work going on and don't forget it was a very big site and they were putting in long concrete runways too.

Incidentally, my father had worked for the local gas company before the war and one of his jobs was to light the gas lamps in the street. Anyway, he was now working for the Air Ministry, in the boiler house at Ibsley. This supplied all the heating and hot water for the base.

I think my dad was too old to join the services so we were both now doing vital work on airfield construction. I know he was involved with the Home Guard.

By now rationing was in force and we did not have too much food. From time to time though, the commanding officer at Ibsley would give us a chitty which allowed us to have some foodstuffs and take them home to the family.

Apart from rationing there was always a shortage of fuel. One of my jobs was to go out and borrow horses and carts from the local farms and we used these in the course of our work, sometimes instead of or in addition to the trucks.

I remember once having to go in to Fordingbridge, about 3 miles from Ibsley, to collect 10 gallons of petrol by horse and cart. We hired in lorries from places like Bournemouth and Poole because the contractors didn't have many vehicles themselves and it was such a big job we always needed extra transport.

When I was at Ibsley Rank Films, I think it was, came down to the site with lots of lorries and vans and so on to make a film called *The First of the Few*. They kept themselves to themselves on the far side of the site near the main Salisbury Road. We had nothing to do with them and although the word went round that famous stars like David Niven were being filmed there, we were far too busy to stop or take any notice. I know they used some of the Spitfires that had flown in to Ibsley. They used the Polish pilots I think. Don't forget, the airfield was being used long before it had been finished so there was always a lot of comings and goings of planes and crews, so we got used to it.

Looking back it seems very strange that they would make a film on a partially completed active airfield, in wartime, but the film was a piece of morale boosting to 'keep the flag flying'. It went to America under the title of *Spitfire* and was used to tell the people there what it was like in England under fire.

We had Spitfires and Hurricanes to begin with and later, when the American Air Force arrived, there were Lockheed Lightnings. They were really interesting aircraft.

We got on well with the RAF chaps. They were always cheerful and didn't seem that worried or nervous about the job they had to do. When the Yanks came they were so friendly we couldn't believe our luck. They invited us in to their mess to eat, of course they made sure we were OK for food by giving us allowances from their PX, and generally they were over the top on everything. I remember later when they suddenly left Ibsley, the stuff they left behind included record players and coats and some of the chaps went through the rooms and took whatever they wanted. It was what they were allowed to do.

We had some good business going with the Americans because they all wanted bikes to get down into Ringwood or off to Bournemouth and so on. Because there were not enough bikes, some of us organised a cycle building and repair service and it went very well. I often went out on scavenges to get bits of bikes so we could use them to keep the Americans on the road as it were. They used to come into our maintenance building and sort out their needs and have the bikes repaired.

When it got towards D-Day we knew something was going on. The aircraft were going off all the time. They brought in some dummy aircraft made of canvas and wood which from the air was supposed to give the impression that all the aircraft were on the ground. In fact they were off on missions. These dummy aircraft I think were brought in on the back of lorries.

Security didn't seem to be that much different to us because we were known at the base and had our permits anyway. By the time the whole airfield was completed there were six, or maybe it was seven, sites outside the perimeter, that were used for accommodation, stores and so on, and up on the hill was the control bunker. Also, some of the farmhouses were used for accommodating the officers.

Once the wings on the aircraft had been painted, all at the very last minute, we knew the big event was about to happen and then of course we knew for certain when it came on the radio later on. We continued to work on the site because it was an active airfield that needed to be kept going twenty-four hours a day. I was by then involved with mechanical maintenance and later I went down to the plotting centre at the Sopley Radar Site.

One thing I remember from early on was the job I had which was to climb the lighting towers at Hengistbury Head, Christchurch, just to change a bulb!

When the war finished me and some mates had to visit all the local airfields and disconnect the petrol pumps from the bowsers to reduce the risk of fire and so on.

In the woods above Ibsley bunkers can be seen and on land which is now a private farm. Many of the airfield's original buildings remain partially intact and are visible from the road. For a number of years an event organised by the local history society has been held every August on the site, in memory of all those who served at RAF Ibsley.

Despite wartime secrecy, however, everyone knew that Ibsley had become a film set for the movies. Even William Joyce (dubbed by many Lord Haw-Haw), who was broadcasting propaganda from Germany, was aware of Ibsley's fortunes. Joyce had in fact lived in the area before fleeing to Germany because of his anti-Semitic views. One of his contacts, who was active in the Ringwood area, was able to monitor the airfields and military activities in the area. This information was transmitted from the radio installation in his bungalow. Ibsley was often mentioned in Lord Haw-Haw's broadcasts. Some of the local population was rather unnerved by the accuracy of the reports and the fact that there was a traitor in their midst. However, they regarded Haw-Haw with complete contempt. 'It could have been your next door neighbour or a friend. It was a bit unsettling and you had to be on your guard all the time. But we really treated Lord Haw-Haw as a joke,' said a former schoolteacher from Poulner.

Nick Berryman was born in London on 1 September 1922. One of his first jobs was with Barclays Bank, but during the war, after an assignment for the RAF at Weston-super-Mare, he was called up and eventually became a Spitfire pilot, though he also flew other aircraft, including the Walrus and Hurricane. He was stationed at RAF Ibsley.

I can remember it well, almost as though it was yesterday in fact . . . because of course it's the sort of thing you can never ever forget. It was at RAF Ibsley, up in the north of the New Forest, and quite near Fordingbridge. This was to be my first operational squadron. The date was January 1943. I had been flying Hurricanes, and I knew that I could handle a Hurricane very well because I'd got something like a hundred or so hours' flying experience on them. But a Spitfire handled very differently and of course you meet the other chaps, your fellow pilots, in the bar at night and you talk to other guys on the squadron that had flown Spitfires. The first thing they tried to do was to put the fear of God into you by saying, don't do this, don't do that. She stalls 5 miles an hour faster than the Hurricane does, and all this sort of thing, and that was the sort of chat you could expect over a pint of beer. These boys didn't know they were doing it, but by the time you went to bed you were bloody horrified really, at the thought of having to go through it on the Spit, the next morning.

I think in this particular case my CO, a chap by the name of Squadron Leader

Nick Berryman in the
cockpit of his Spitfire.
(Nick Berryman)

Bird-Wilson, said to me 'Okay, go and read the book, Nick, and then when you're happy, we'll get you off on LZX'.

That was the squadron number – 66 Squadron was LZ – and X was the Spitfire designation. It was the first I ever flew. It was actually a Spitfire 5b, with four machine guns and two cannons. And having done what I was told, because you did as you were told in those days, you didn't argue. And I was only just about coming up to being a flying officer, I think, I had got over my pilot officer thing. And anyway I pushed off in the Spit, I used the runway at Ibsley, which is the one that leaves the control tower immediately on your left and goes down south-west towards Mockbeggar Lane. Anyway, I found the take-off was easy enough, to be honest, no different really to flying a Miles Master or even the Hurricane.

So the take-off was fine, undercarriage up, because we didn't use flaps on a Spit as we used to use the flaps on the Hurricane. So it was just undercarriage up, and there I was up into the wide blue yonder – no problem at all.

Then in the next five or six minutes, I got comfortable and happy with the airplane, I turned it left, and I turned it right, I dived it, climbed it and I remember being over Bournemouth, or virtually over Bournemouth, when I decided I'd give the old girl a roll. So I pulled the nose up, and rolled it over, but when I was on my back I didn't get the stick (the control column), far enough forward. It was a different feel to the Hurricane, that was the long and short of it, and with the result that with all the controls being reversed, I, what we called Split S'd out of it, out of this roll. And my nose was going down. I should have had the common sense to roll out of that, but I was very inexperienced, I was very young, and I didn't roll out of it. So I zoomed over Bournemouth at about 200 feet and I could just imagine the crowds below going diving for cover and saying to themselves, 'Oh Christ', you know. But, anyway, I survived, so did the good folk of Bournemouth, and that was the first experience that I had with my LZX.

But it was a delightful airplane to fly and I realised that it was equally as good as the Hurricane, which really quite surprised me. Not that any of us had heard too much at that time how much better the Spitfire was as a fighter, but only as a fighter, was it better than the Hurricane.

So anyway, I took her back to Ibsley and lined up with the runway and got permission to land, I think the old control tower had given me a call sign, and it was Lucas One Seven – 'you have permission to land' and I called in, and I made my approach, got me wheels down and realising that, from the night before, over a pint, I'd got to make the approach at about eighty, I added 5 miles an hour for me. That made it 85. Then I thought of my Mum and I added 5 miles an hour for my Mum. So I came over the edge at about 90. Of course, any Spitfire pilots reading this interview will immediately start to giggle because a Spit will float and float and float. But anyway, there was I, halfway along the runway and still hadn't got down after the second bounce, and I thought I'd better go round again. However, once again realising what I'd heard the night before that the flaps when raised on a Spit would drop you like a stone for two hundred feet – and they did. So, the landing procedures on a Spit was wheels down, undercarriage down, and then get your flaps down. So down came the flaps – 'sccchweep' – like that and they gave me a bit more lift, slowed me up a little bit, but I'm still floating halfway up the runway and I thought to myself – 'I'd better go round again' – but I didn't, I sat there like a frightened chicken and decided that no way was I going to climb this untried engine, as far as I was concerned, to climb to 200 feet before I put my flaps up again, to drop like a stone as I'd been told the night before.

However, I got it down and started to roll. Now just at that time, in January 1943, the runway was being extended, and suddenly with my tail down, but still rolling very fast, I saw a lot of Irish workmen throwing their picks and shovels and all their digging instruments in all directions, and fleeing for dear life. So this idiot, then, in a Spitfire, sailed past them at a great rate of knots and finally ended up no more than 5 or 10 yards from the far edge. That area now, having been back to Ibsley, is used for a sort of yard for business, and I believe that's where the runway was being extended at the time of my little incident. All I can say on looking back is thank God for Nick Berryman alone.

Going back right to the beginning, though, I started flying and was trained in the United States. The United States at that time were taking British boys, to give them some flying training and that was the American way of saying – Well, we are on your side, but we can't be seen to be – because they weren't in the war until later. So, a lot of us were put on a troopship, we crossed the Atlantic, and the Americans started to train us. So I went straight in to Maxwell Field, Alabama, where I went through another six or seven weeks initial training, which got up most of our noses because the British boys at that time, they'd been through an awful lot of bombing in London, and the big cities. We didn't want to march to breakfast with a full band at 6 o'clock in the morning, which is what we were having to do as part of the protocol on base. But, anyway, we did it and then I went on to Arcadia, Florida, where I flew the PT17 for the first of my flights.

Of course there was the odd chap or two that couldn't cope at all and then he was quickly washed out. But then the wash-out rate was tremendously high, it was something like 60 per cent, and those of us that were washed out became navigators and gunners. That didn't mean to say that we weren't any good at anything, we were just considered not suitable as pilots.

Now this happened to me, because on the PT17 I did forty-nine hours and twenty-five minutes flying. That number of hours indelibly printed on my brain, and the instructor, who is an immaculately dressed lieutenant with his beautiful brown jacket, with two bars on his shoulders, pink hue trousers and one of those soft peaked caps, said 'Mister, I wanna give you a check ride'. So I said, 'okay, sir', and I climbed into this PT17 and he said 'I'd like you to give me a steep turn to the left, please, and a steep turn to the right, please'. And I did all this through these 'gosport tubes' that came through your ears, you know. And I thought I was getting on fine and then he said 'Er, would you give me a precautionary landing'. Well, a precautionary landing, of course, is to drop the airplane as near to the hedge as you possibly can. Well, it floated and floated, I was good at floating airplanes, I think. I put it down on the deck and he climbed out of this airplane and I shall never, never forget it.

He moved his goggles from his eyes, up to his forehead. He put his hands on his hips, and he said, in a booming and drawling American accent, 'Mister, you's never gonna fly an airplane as long as you's got a hole in your ass!' That was me finished.

As far as the United States Air Corps were concerned, they didn't need me, they were looking for West Pointers, they were looking for blokes that were very much brighter than I was at the time – I was a bank clerk and they didn't need me, but a while later I was lucky enough to find myself sitting at the Court of Inquiry alongside a guy called Arthur Rhys. Now Arthur Rhys was a big man in many many ways. Anybody that knows anything about rugger would know the name A.M. Rhys. He was capped for Wales, he was capped for the Metropolitan Police, he was capped for Cambridge and he was a man that stood 10 feet taller than most. Twenty-eight years of age at that time, I was nineteen. Anyway, he went into the Court of Inquiry first, to be told he was being washed out, and he came up with a salute and the blokes in charge said, 'We're washing you out, Mr Rhys', because they always called you Mister over there.

Okay and so Mr Rhys was washed out, but before he stood down he said, addressing the panel in his very distinct Welsh accent, 'If you think', he said, 'I come all this bloody way to be told I can't fly an airplane after twenty-five bloody hours,

you're bloody wrong.' With that he came up with a salute, turned about and walked
out. And the panel sat absolutely dumbfounded at this blatant impertinence you see.
Then they called me in, and I went in as a rather innocent nineteen-year-old and I
came up with a salute and I said 'And that's how I feel too.' When I think about that
now, the hairs stand up on the back of my neck. The cheek of it really.

And we were the first British boys ever to be transferred to a unit, to a British
flying training school, which had just started, in the United States. And the United
States by that time had just come into the war. So in the January I went across to
Texas with Arthur Rhys and we carried on our flying with a course that had just
started. Fortunately, but no surprise to us, we both passed out very well. Arthur
Rhys went on to fly Mustangs and survived the war and I believe only died about
eighteen months ago, God bless him. I came back to fly the Spitfires and the
Hurricanes and finally the Walrus Amphibian.

I was flying the Spitfire for the whole of 1943, from start to finish in some shape
or form, interspersed with one mad moment when I was flying the Boulton Paul
Defiant. But otherwise it was the Spitfires for the whole of 1943.

Now the Spitfire is regarded as a wonderful plane to fly and I will tell you
my opinion of it, shall I? Oh yes, it was a delightful airplane, it was, in the old
fashioned sense, a gay airplane to fly. It was light, it was a fun airplane. The
Hurricane, too, was a fun airplane. But the Hurricane had a gentle solidity that the
Spitfire somehow didn't. The Spitfire was like chasing the prettiest schoolgirl up
the street, when you're eighteen years of age, and the Hurricane was like chasing a
twenty-eight-year-old sprinter, if you know what I mean. It was a bit different!

But it was just delightful, and of course very proficient at its job. Which was as
a fighter, whereas the Hurricane wasn't. Although the Hurricane was considered
a fighter in its early days, it was by that time being used for rocket firing, and it
was the forerunner of the Typhoon. And it was a nice sturdy airplane, was the
Hurricane, and yes, I liked it very much.

Of all the sorties that Nick Berryman flew from Ibsley, there is one in particular
that stands out in his mind as being exciting as well as dangerous.

Well, the dangerous bit I think was being upside down 200 feet over Bournemouth.
. . . But our job on 66 Squadron at that time was taking the Flying Fortresses to St
Nazaire, Larouillies, Brest. And it was quite a shaker for me the first time to sit in
that rather bleak squadron hut, and, as a new boy, to watch the other boys going off
for the first time as we were expected to do. And being told to take all identification
out of our pockets and all our money out of our pockets and then we were sort of
thrust into the air and then we were flying with the Fortresses when they carried out
raids against St Nazaire, Brest and Lorient. And I did nothing with 66 Squadron
from Ibsley other than escort the Forts and bombers of any type – I was escort, then.
I remember this very well too. I was told that I was going to sleep in a farmhouse.
Where that farmhouse was, I don't know. I have tried to find the house we were

in but as yet I have not been successful. Anyway, all the other 66 boys were there and I was given a bed and told that that was Flying Officer Berryman's room.

The bed I can assure you was very damp, and when I say damp, it was terribly damp. But the whole farmhouse was wringing wet, and it was January. And I remember going into dinner one night and you were expected, in those days, to at least come out of your flying kit and get into your number one uniform, you know. Of course there were extreme circumstances when you didn't do that. But when you could you were expected to change and be clean. I remember walking in and got half a pint of beer and I'd got a real stinker of a cold at the time, through a damp bed. I stood in front of the fire and I was surrounded in steam as my uniform dried out. It had been hanging on this Ibsley farmhouse wall for probably thirty-six hours so it was soaking, more than just damp. And the steam just rose off me, just came off me like a cloud.

But apart from that, the fun of being at Ibsley was tremendous because the boss, Bird-Wilson, was a good boss and he had a dog, which we all loved and treated almost as our own I suppose. I think it was something like a terrier – bit of a bull terrier. And then of course we all used to go down to the pub at night when we were on stand-down, and we'd go down to – is it called the 'Broad Beams'* or something like that?

Anyway, it's only just down the road, and I see it from time to time. In fact I went over to lunch there about two years ago and all the memories came flooding back. And we used to meet in that pub as a squadron and then we'd drink our pints of beer. We didn't drink a lot you know – there are stories about we used to drink a great deal, but we didn't – certainly there were nights when we'd get stood down and then we'd get a bit tanked up, but in the main we didn't drink a great deal, and we were only youngsters.

Aircraft flying from Ibsley at that time, in the main, were Spitfires during that January, February, March, April time. There were Spitfires, Spitfires and more Spitfires, but the Whirlwinds used to fly in and out from 263 Squadron. They were a delightful airplane to fly up 'alongside'. Unfortunately, I lost a good friend flying Whirlwinds and he's commemorated in the memorial garden at the Tangmere Aviation Museum.

But the Whirlwinds were there and 504 Squadron I remember were very much implicated in their escort work which, in the main, was low-level escort work. They were always on shipping. Then there were the Typhoons, which used to fly in and out. But, from memory, they only flew in and out and I can't remember the Typhoons ever being based there.

Nick went on to recall general life in the RAF:

As a serving officer in the RAF during the war – and this is only a personal opinion, my interpretation, I was never the slightest bit frightened. The attitude was, it won't

---

* The Old Beams – still a popular pub to this day!

be me – it might be this guy, but not me. I suppose that was one of the advantages of being young. What I was aware of was the tremendous camaraderie amongst pilots. Of course there was and had to be trust, and I'll also use the word love. There was a tremendous affection between all of us. It was unfortunate in many ways that sergeants and non-commissioned were often separated, well, they were separated from officers because of the messing arrangements. As a young pilot or flying officer, I was always in officers' messes. My contemporaries and the guys that I would fly with were very often flight sergeants, sergeants and warrant officers. So I didn't always have the privilege of spending drinking time with the guys that I would fly with. But we were together all day long, and we treated each other as complete and utter equals.

I was Nick. The chap over there was Ted, he was a warrant officer – didn't matter. The tremendous trust between you was remarkable. It goes even deeper than that for me because I was trained with two other guys, one by the name of Roger McCobser, the other one Flight Lieutenant McNarre Taylor. These two blokes were quite remarkable in their own way. Well, the story with Roger McCobser is fascinating. He was a Frenchman and he escaped from France and got into England and eventually married a girl called Valerie. So that's when I first knew him, and then later he joined 197 Squadron, which was a Typhoon Squadron that eventually ended up at Tangmere. Valerie and Roger were only married for three months when he was killed flying the Hawk Typhoon. The guy that put the body down the hole and saluted as it was buried in the city of Lincoln was Ray McNarre Taylor, the other friend. He met Valerie, the widow, and in time married her. He was a particularly good friend of mine was Ray McNarre Taylor, and I was delighted some year later, no, not a year later, some three months later, to be invited to be the best man at his wedding because he was going to marry the widow.

So I was best man and then when their baby son was born I became godfather. Unfortunately, the marriage lasted just one year, because poor Ray was killed flying a Spitfire. And he ended up in an unknown grave because he hit another Spitfire on a sortie and disappeared in the ogin (sea).

So Valerie was widowed for the second time. I was in the Middle East by this time and I wrote to her. I was shattered a bit by the loss of two good friends. Of course Valerie (a nice woman whom I'd met a couple of times) was not only a widow but was bringing up the boy on her own. The lad had no father after just three months. Such is the pain of war.

And when I got back I went to see her because she was looking after the dog that Ray and I had bought together, a springer spaniel. I went to get the dog because I was to look after it. I met Valerie again, fell in love with her and married her – I'd got nothing else to do at the time you know!

So, yes there was love among fighter pilots, and loyalty. And those two boys, my son now, who became a fighter pilot in the Royal Air Force and his half-brother – they are, I am pleased to say, the very best of friends. It's really wonderful to see them together. And when I sometimes look at the two boys together, I don't see my two boys, I see Ray McNarre Taylor and me – at the same age.

That's my story, and I hope you get some idea of life in those times and the way we were in those dark yet memorable days in our history.

5

Typhoon Tales

James Kyle is a legendary and respected ex-Typhoon pilot who flew from Needs Ore Point, near Beaulieu. Military artist John Batchelor painted his Typhoon, and the island of Mauritius produced a stamp featuring the aircraft. Jimmy took part in the victory flypast over London alongside Douglas Bader, in 1945.

James (Jimmy) Kyle was born in Motherwell, Scotland, in September 1922, and after a public school education he became an apprentice engineer. Volunteering for the Royal Air Force, he undertook flying training in Texas and then became a member of 197 Typhoon Fighter Squadron, based at Drem. Jimmy was awarded the Distinguished Flying Medal in 1944.

One particular aircraft he flew, the Hawker Typhoon 1B JP 682 of 197 Squadron RAF, gained something of a celebrity status. Since the war it has been featured many times in magazines and paintings.

From his early career in the RAF James was to win fame and one of his earliest memories is his friendship with Clark Gable, who served in the USAAF. James joined the RAF in December 1941. He first flew Steermans and eventually Harvards in May 1942. Upon his return to England James flew the Hurricane, Typhoon and Tempest.

James Kyle. *(James Kyle)*

In 1944 197 Squadron moved from Tangmere to the Advanced Landing Ground at Needs Ore Point.

Jimmy takes up the story at a significant time in his career and during a turning point in the fortunes of war for the Allied nations.

It really is as clear as day to me. It's as though it happened only yesterday but as the

James (second from left) and fellow pilots, *c.* 1942. *(James Kyle)*

years pass my story is almost like a dream. I know it happened but the world has moved on so much and sixty years after the events it is difficult to realise the reality.

During the month of April 1944 our squadron, 197, was moved from Tangmere, in Sussex, just along the coast into Hampshire, to a temporary advanced landing ground (ALG) at Needs Ore Point. This was an area of farmland running down to the New Forest coastline along the edge of the Solent. Two large fields were taken over and combined to form a decent sized base, and a runway was made out of prefabricated summerfeld steel tracking.

The farmhouse, still there today, was taken over as operations and anti-aircraft batteries surrounded the site.

There were now four squadrons under canvas, with a mobile tactical and intelligence headquarters. These were 257, 266, 193 and of course 197. It was pretty rough and ready on this site, but it was comfortable for what we needed, we had good food and access to a single shower somewhere. We used to go out on armed Rhubarb/Recces, staying at between 2,000 and 3,000 feet at a cruising speed of 300 mph. Our objective was to search, bomb, strafe and generally cause havoc against military targets. The Typhoons were fitted with a 500-lb bomb, and we had a long-range fuel tank. I hit many good targets, you know, trains, tanks and potentially explosive targets. I had some good results, I can tell you.

After one particularly successful action when we accounted for a lot of targets destroyed including several ME109s, we started the celebrations early

James Kyle, one of the Brylcreem boys.
(James Kyle)

at the local hotel in Beaulieu and continued when we got back to our tented city.

I remember two incidents in particular from my time at Needs Ore Point. Going back to the way the airfield was set out: the tracking was laid straight on the fields. Its steel mesh plates and sheeting were laid on the ground, and the 'ups and downs' of the uneven surface really caused difficulties for our Typhoon aircraft, on take-off and landing. The propeller of the Typhoon is, as you know, quite large, and with the aircraft tail up, on take-off, the prop had only 9 inches clearance from the runway surface.

The legendary Typhoon.
(*James Kyle*)

On one occasion two aircraft were scrambled for a sortie and in the rush to get airborne the leading aircraft's nose was pushed too far forward as it thundered down the length of the temporary runway. I am afraid that the inevitable happened. The scene unravelled before our eyes. The propeller dug into the steel tracking on one of the bumps in the field and the Typhoon first somersaulted, then cartwheeled, and then sadly crashed and splintered into hundreds of large and small pieces as it still continued careering down the field. The second aircraft was taking off in what is called cross formation, but it was unable to avoid the debris being flung about as a result of the crash of the first aircraft. The second Typhoon 'cannoned' into the first aircraft, straight into the fire and flying metal, smashing up and adding to the already horrifying sight. The two aircraft were, of course, totally destroyed and yet two more brave pilots lost their lives.

Myself and my fellow pilots, and the ground crews, stood shocked, aghast and speechless as we surveyed the horrible scene and were numbed at the thought of the pilots. However, the temporary runway was quickly cleared of strewn wreckage and shortly afterwards two replacement aircraft took off in a delayed answer to the original scramble.

Jimmy was witness to an action that was to become something of a mystery in later years and was referred to in Nevil Shute's book *Requiem for a Wren*, which chronicles aspects of military life.

During the same month as that terrible crash on the airfield, on 18 April 1944, just a month or two before D-Day, two squadrons took off from the advanced landing ground at Needs Ore Point to patrol south of the Isle of Wight. We had it on good authority that something was afoot. We had been airborne for about fifteen minutes or so and we were circling some 20 miles out to sea. Suddenly, in the distance to the east of the island, a formation of German aircraft was sighted as they made an approach for the English coast. Naturally we turned to give chase. The German formation wheeled away and eluded us, turning eastward towards France, and then out of range.

One lone aircraft, however, seemingly unaware of our existence, was later observed flying straight and level, slogging slowly and earnestly inwards towards the shores of the south coast. Within a short space of time that medium bomber, a Ju188, very unlucky to find a Typhoon squadron airborne, was lying in a horrible wreck in a field on the edge of the Exbury estate, close to the Solent and a stone's throw from our base at Needs Ore.

Our squadron landed and we were taken to view the wreckage. I have never witnessed such a mass of destruction, death and damage at close range. My fellow pilots and I stood speechless. There was nothing hostile in our shared silence as we gazed at the appalling sight before us.

The Junkers 188 normally flew with a crew of four. However, at a glance it was obvious that this aircraft had more than four dead bodies entangled among the bits and pieces of its broken frame. The human remains were picked up and I am afraid literally shovelled aboard an open lorry in a dreadfully mangled mess. The bodies were transported by tumbrel back to the medical centre, which was a marquee, well away from our domestic site. There the remains were unloaded, and a number of us watched stoically as a well-built, rather red-faced local police sergeant proceeded to handle formless pieces, which were placed together, as they slid off the tilted lorry.

Enveloped in an odious smell, this country bobby rearranged these portions of raw flesh and broken bones, which protruded through the skin, in an attempt to complete whole bodies. He succeeded, an incredible seven times over. The only thing alive and ticking was the watch of the Junkers pilot. It was later reported that the aircraft and its seven crew members were defecting,* but unfortunately they were unlucky to have selected such an inopportune [*sic*] moment, at the time when this country was on high alert just ahead of the start of the D–Day campaign.

Returning from an early morning raid on Abbeville, I was invited to report to Air Vice-Marshal McEvoy, who was waiting for me in the officers' mess marquee. He asked me a lot of detailed questions about my operational experiences. As a result of that meeting, and a while later, I was promoted and subsequently moved my belongings from one tent to another. Now, as Pilot Officer Kyle, I entered the fascinating world of the officers' mess.

On the morning of 6 June 1944 I climbed out of bed at 4.30 a.m. It was dark of course, windy and very wet. Two squadrons of fully armed Typhoons taxied out for take-off and by 6.15 a.m. my fellow pilots and I were airborne.

Our target was Normandy, the small town of Bayeux in fact. We set off at 900 feet, in poor conditions. We knew this was the big thing. The aircraft now had striped painted wings. Below us in the Solent and out into the Channel were ships, thousands of them. It looked as though the Isle of Wight was being towed out to sea. We witnessed the mighty naval bombardment of the French coast. D-Day had begun!

Our target was a German High Command headquarters, located in a château, and this we bombed with little opposition. I continued to support the D-Day operations with rhubarbs and ramrods, all successful, and various 'beat ups'. For some thirty days after 6 June we operated from Needs Ore Point and from nearby Hurn airfield (now Bournemouth International Airport) and then we went to

---

*The circumstances still remain a mystery amid much speculation.

advance bases B15 and B3 on the actual beachheads.

Those are my memories of Needs Ore Point and the New Forest: an amazing time in my life.

6

Pylewell's War Effort

The Teynham family estate at Pylewell Park, near Lymington, was requisitioned for a variety of military purposes, including the construction of Pylewell Airfield (also known as Lymington) for the D-Day campaign. It was a temporary, two-runway airfield overlooking the Solent. A few buildings and various other reminders can still be seen around the estate. What was the debriefing room remains, as does part of the fuel depot. Cottages and houses close by accommodated troops and were used for the provision of support services. Well hidden now are parts of a P-47 Thunderbolt aircraft which hang from a tree on the estate. The remains of an antenna system, used

The south façade of Pylewell House.
(Author's collection)

for base communications, also hangs in one of the trees just outside Pylewell House. When the Americans vacated the house, they 'just cut the wires' and left the antenna system dangling high up in the tree.

A plaque has been erected nearby, close to an original Blister hangar, and this briefly tells the story of Pylewell airfield. Several gatherings of American veterans have taken place at Pylewell since the war.

John Roper-Curzon (now Lord Teynham) still lives in the family home at Pylewell Park. At the outbreak of war the estate employed twenty-five gardeners and about twenty indoor staff. Today the estate of 2,000 acres is occasionally open to the public during the spring and summer as part of the National Gardens Scheme.

Lord Teynham recalls that as a young boy he felt he could reach out from his bedroom window and almost touch the tail-fins of the 50th Fighter Group Republic Thunderbolts parked up on one of the dispersal areas on the estate. He also remembers being stopped at the gated entrance to the cottage where he then lived. 'A huge giant of an American GI checked my ID card every time I left and returned to the cottage.'

He describes some of his earliest memories of Pylewell during the war:

Lord Teynham, aged twelve. *(Lord Teynham)*

One of the first things to happen here at Pylewell was that this house was requisitioned by the War Department, as it was called then. It was, to begin with, mainly used as barracks and they put, I think it was the Royal Northumberland Fusiliers – well they weren't Royal then, they were just the Northumberland Fusiliers, they later became the Royal Northumberland Fusiliers. They were quartered here and the gardens actually became the first battle camp in England. I think later, when it was dismantled, it was transferred and became the School of Infantry at Warminster.

But meanwhile the house was requisitioned and we all had to get out. And the family all moved, temporarily, up to the Home Farmhouse in the village.

There was by now a lot of activity. I seem to remember the Germans used what were known as incendiaries, which were really large bombs that let out a whole lot of smaller firebombs. Fortunately they didn't land on the house, but I can remember fire bombs smouldering away all over the garden. My grandmother, who was really quite undaunted by the war and what was going on here, used to go out in her mink coat and her white kid gloves with her maid and with a dustpan and brush and a can

Training on the Pylewell Estate was varied, but intense.
(Lord Teynham)

of water. They were trying to sweep up these bombs, and every time the maid poured water on them they used to flare up because they were magnesium. It was all very fascinating and exciting I have to say, even looking back after all these years.

The other thing, extraordinary at the time, was when we went up the road leading up to the gardens here on the estate. There were thousands of strips of silver paper lying on the ground, which we later discovered were dropped by the Germans to confuse our coastal radar. So we gathered these up and used them for decoration on the Christmas tree, because you couldn't get the proper tinsel in those days of course.

I think it was about that time that the local defence volunteers were formed, later of course they were to become the Home Guard. And their main duty, believe it or not, was looking for German parachutists and spies. They were under the command of an old gentleman, well, they were all old gentlemen really – a real 'Dads' Army'. Anyway they were under the command of an old boy called Gaston Du Pesse who lived at Newtown Park, which was the next big house to here. By the way, his house was taken over in the war. It was used to house all the contents of the *Queen Mary* – extraordinary!

Anyway, the Home Guard were very active in the village. They set up barricades made of barbed wire and bits of wood and that sort of thing. But because of the blackout motorists couldn't see where they were going, and I remember that there was one old lady who crashed into their best barricade and completely smashed it to pieces.

Also, the Home Guard locally had a couple of dugouts, which they constructed out of an old metal buoy, which was washed up on the shore. They cut it in half and made two dugouts.

The war seemed to go on a bit like that for some time, and my grandmother decided that it was time to have an air-raid shelter – to tell you the truth she never went into it because it filled with water. What's funny is, I think she won the prize for the best private air-raid shelter in Hampshire. Can you believe it? It was noted for having two entrances and we used to tease her that the second entrance was really the servants' entrance. But it was well stocked with food and drink and stuff, tins of biscuits, ham; relations had sent over a lot of it from Canada. Oh, she could have withstood a siege for years down in this shelter.

A little time after that my mother and my brother and I were moved into Lisle Court, which is another house here on the estate, in fact just a little further along the shore. And we were there really until the end of the war. There was a huge amount of activity going on at the time, and as we approached the invasion time and D-Day in mid-1944, there were an increasing number of tanks and guns, and all the roads around here and across the Forest had to be widened with concrete strips – even now you can see them – and lay-bys were made as hard-standings, such as those near here in the village at Pilley.

The woods around here were full of troops and the Lymington river nearby was a scene of great activity. There were minesweepers there, fast motor-boats too. The

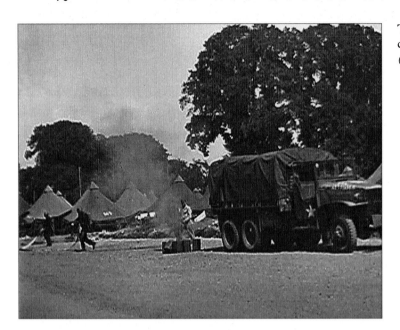

The area surrounding Pylewell was
dense with troops under canvas.
(Hampshire Fire & Rescue Service)

Solent was beginning to fill up, chock-a-block – you could almost have walked
across to the island [Isle of Wight]. There were hundreds, thousands of ships out
there. And of course we could see all this, and there was a submarine net, a sort
of gate really, at each end of the Solent. (Sowley Boom close to Lepe Beach has
only recently been removed.) And they would open this gate to let ships in and
then shut it behind them. Fascinating! And the Germans were constantly trying
to lay mines, and on a still night I can remember hearing the noise of the German
E-Boats. They would come up to, you know, where the Needles are, and drop their
mines. And the minesweepers would then go and sweep them up.

However, I think the airfield was really the most important thing here. That was
constructed in only six weeks early in '44. (This was ALG 551.) I think that must
have been about the end of February or March, but I can't remember exactly. And
in order to have it ready and operational very quickly they laid a steel mesh runway.
In fact there were two runways, one going from Lisle Court Farm up to Portmore,
that's north and south. And the other one, which was for the prevailing wind, from
north-east to south-west, went right across the park here at Pylewell. That was very
sad because they cut down all our oak trees, in fact they cut a whole wood down to
get the runway right through.

For me it was fascinating – by this time I was aged fifteen – and I spent a lot of
time watching the frantic activity. It was the Americans who were here and they were
very kind, especially to the children. We used to lean over the gate and they used
to give us sweets – they called it 'candy', I think. But they couldn't understand our
curious ways . . . how civilians could be living in the middle of an airfield in what
they thought was the front line – they simply could not understand that.

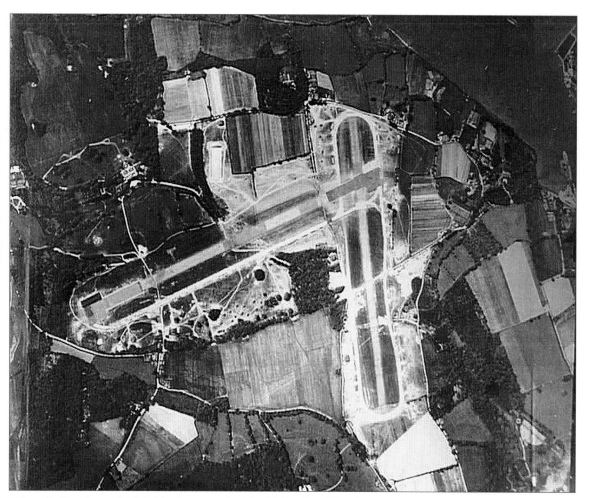

Pylewell (Lymington) airfield, photographed in 1944. *(Lord Teynham)*

There were two people whom the commanding officer came to see my mother about one day. He asked 'Who were these people?' Well, one of them was our gardener, who was a very distinguished gentleman, a Mr Snellgrove, who had been in former years a forest keeper. He used to come to work in a marvellous green uniform, with brass buttons, highly polished, and leggings. He was very distinguished looking, white-haired and had a long drooping white moustache. He'd come up to one of the American barriers and they'd say, 'You can't go any further' and he'd say, 'You can't keep me waiting, because I have to work for her ladyship'. And they were so dumbfounded, particularly when he just lifted his bicycle over the barricade and bicycled up to the house.

There was another individual who lived in a cottage down by Lisle Court: she was called Miss Wood, and she really was something from another age altogether.

The Ship Inn, Lymington. *(Author's collection)*

The Lymington River was full of naval craft in 1944. *(Author's collection)*

She also had an antiquated bicycle, and she wore billowing skirts and long white gloves. A Miss Marple figure perhaps. And the Americans just couldn't believe that such a person existed.

Anyhow, the next thing I seem to remember was the minesweepers. They were moored out there in the Solent. My father, Captain the Lord Teynham DSO, DSE, was the captain in charge of all the minesweeping forces between here and the Normandy beaches. What a responsibility! He kept a lot of minesweepers in the Lymington river. And he also took over the Ship Inn that is still down on Lymington Quay as his base and headquarters.

Anyway, one day when the ships were moored here out on the Solent, a hail of bullets shot into the air over the ships and the crews all had to go down below decks. Well, it was the Americans test firing the guns on their Thunderbolt planes on the airfield here at Pylewell. They thought it was quite safe to fire into the Solent, but what an oversight. It wasn't safe at all. The Navy then complained, and they, for some extraordinary reason, did it through my mother. They thought she'd have some influence. So she went to see the American commanding officer. The Americans were so apologetic and they immediately set about building an enormous mound of earth. And I can remember it being constructed by the first bulldozer I'd ever seen, a Caterpillar obviously flown in especially from America. This huge mound was built and thereafter they fired into the mound and all was well.

Did John remember the aircraft at Pylewell?

Oh yes, the aircraft here were Thunderbolts, which I think were fighter-bombers. They were here for a few weeks just before D-Day and gradually they stepped up activity, by going up every day. We would hear them, the engines warming up, from as early as 5.30 in the morning.

And there was a remarkable old man, a Mr Roe from the nearby village of East End, who ran a bakery. And he would come over here at 5.30 in the morning, in a horse and cart, with lovely fresh baked bread, and he would serve this to the American pilots before they set off. And they would, I suppose, set off about 6 in the morning and they might do two or even three sorties over to France and back. There was one particular plane, and on it was painted a blonde wearing black silk stockings. Most of the aircraft had paintings on their noses, it was traditional. And I think my mother had befriended this particular young pilot and when he flew over our house, he would always dip the aircraft wings and he would wave out of the cockpit, and we would all wave back. One day he didn't come back and so my mother went along to look at his normal parking space, which was just over the hedge behind our house. She enquired about the pilot, and she was told that he'd been shot down, and I know my mother had always wondered who he was, what his name was.

This is all rather extraordinary, because a few years ago, that was the time when there was the fiftieth anniversary of D-Day, we had lots of the American veterans visiting the site here. It was a lovely day, the weather was kind and we gave them all lunch outside in the gardens. And I was talking about this particular plane with the mascot on it, the one that my mother talked about and one of these veterans, I think he was called Franklyn S. Coyle or something, suddenly wrote to me upon his return to America, and said I've researched this story and I can now tell you the name of the young man. His name was Pressley C. Chapman of 313 Squadron . . . he was shot down on a mission, bombing a railway siding at Le Manoir, south-east of Rouen.

When D-Day came we were over at the farmyard just at the end of the drive where they did the debriefing. We were able to hear straight, first hand, exactly how they were getting on and how many miles they'd advanced inland. You'd rush back to the wireless and you heard what that had got to say, so it was a fascinating time.

Apart from that apparent lapse of security, that we could hear the debriefings, the general security was very, very strict, in fact stricter and stricter as time went on. And you had to have a pass to get everywhere. We were allowed in or out of this area, or not as the case may be. This actually pleased my brother and me because we couldn't go to school, which was very nice, and we stayed here and we had marvellous stories to tell our school friends when we went back to school later in the year, in September, the next term that was.

As I said before, security was very strict as we neared D-Day. The extraordinary thing was everybody living here knew what was going to happen. We also knew it wouldn't be on 4 June, because there was a tremendous gale blowing, so everybody knew it wouldn't be that night. And then the next two days, as the gale died down, we thought 'this is it'. My mother walked along the lane where she saw the most secret thing of all, which was the black and white stripes painted on the underneath and on the fuselage and the wings of the American planes. Here it was done at the very last minute although I have been told that the painting of aeroplanes was

The site of the former debriefing centre, Pylewell airfield.
(Author's collection)

done at different times at different airfields. This was of course the new Allied identification. We knew that was it was going to happen and sure enough it was, and we saw the ships moving off.

At that stage of the war I think we really had complete air superiority. And not a single German plane came over. At night-time the siren would sometimes go off, but really that didn't usually mean anything to us. But the Americans here were still all fairly green about such things, they were really quite terrified and they dug themselves foxholes. I think they mainly came from Texas. They had different calls, according to what part of Texas they came from, and you could hear them, calling from one hole, to another hole, and if others called back in the same tongue, they felt reassured, that sort of thing. In some respects they were also rather casual, we thought. You know, if they'd got bombs still on board after returning from France, they'd just drop them. They actually dropped one or two near some of the minesweepers parked in the Lymington river. They just didn't think, but I suppose that having rivers and so on full of ships was such a unique situation the dangers may not have been immediately apparent.

When the ships disappeared from the Solent and Lymington river and the airplanes disappeared from the fields outside the Teynham family home, what was the atmosphere like?

Oh, well, the general feeling was that the war had rather passed over us and gone away, and although on still nights you could hear the guns in France, Normandy of course, we felt that we were all going to get back to normal. I think we did up to a certain point. But of course rationing was very strict then, even more strict. I mean, you got two ounces of sugar, two ounces of jam, four pennyworth of meat per week. That's all you got. Well, I think that was it. And the planes all went, the Pylewell airfield closed down and for us it was really the end of the war. The airfield closed after just a few weeks although other airfields in the Forest were active for longer.

The house continued to be requisitioned because the Americans were still here. They were nothing to do with the airfield, they were a separate body altogether. And when they left we then had Italian prisoners of war. Well, they had absolutely no desire to escape, they were perfectly happy and looked after the place quite well. They had to stay until the war was over; it went on for another year in Europe. I think they stayed on a bit after that, I can't really remember.

John Teynham recalls the 1940s at Lisle Court as being particularly exciting.

Three things stand out in my mind. One was being woken up in the night by a tremendous noise, and going to the window and looking out seeing Southampton in flames. It's 20 miles away, but you could see it, it was unbelievable. The whole sky was lit up, there were searchlight beams and you could see the German planes caught in the beam. Anti-aircraft going up, everything, anti-aircraft fire, you know, shells bursting, tremendous noise. This must have been early in 1940 when the first raids took place.

There were two other things. One was my brother and me and our mother I suppose, we were playing on the front lawn. And I remember seeing, coming in from the sea, an airplane flying very low and quite fast, straight towards us. My mother, very protective, shovelled us indoors, pretty quick. It was just as well because just as we got into the house we heard his machine guns going, and it machine-gunned right across the lawn, you could see where the bullets had gone. That was one incredible thing.

The other thing happened on a glorious afternoon. We were all out on the lawn and the Germans were bombing Portsmouth, I think. And then the siren had gone, but nothing happened here. And I can remember seeing very, very high up in the east a German plane had been hit by our anti-aircraft fire. I believe it was the highest flying aircraft ever shot down by anti-aircraft fire, and you saw it coming down like a leaf. And the next thing the engine came out – I suppose it was the engine, something black with black smoke. And it went down much faster than the plane. I believe it landed near Lee-on-Solent.

I think those were the three things that really stood out at that time. It was very exciting, and also frightening of course. But to us it was thrilling, really.

There are still signs of the military activity of those far off years in the park today.

There are bits of wire – you know the runway was made of steel mesh and wire. Some of it still sticks out of the ground in places and the farmers and sometimes their ploughs get tangled in it. There's one hangar still up the road here. You can

see it just off the road to Lymington.*

And one or two little brick buildings, and the farm buildings where they had debriefings, but apart from that it's all gone now, and we've replanted the wood,

This once-derelict Blister hangar has now been renovated. *(Author's collection)*

* This has been renovated and is used today.

which you may remember they chopped down to make the runways. There are also wires from their radio systems up in the trees at the bottom of the garden and bits of the wreck of an Allied aircraft down on the foreshore.

7

The Secret Forest

In the years before the outbreak of the Second World War Britain had a very active Intelligence Service. For some time the government had been very well informed of what was happening on mainland Europe and, in particular, in Germany. Facts were known about Germany's military preparedness, of her extensive precautions against raids from the air and of her efforts to prepare, in secret, a huge war machine.

Clues were many and obvious though, not only to those members of the Intelligence Services who were witnessing these events from inside Germany, but also to a number of alert politicians and academics in England, for example, youth organisations were being formed, there was a concerted effort to develop physical training as a basic requirement, the labour corps was being expanded and so too was the number of Civilian Flying Schools.

The public in Britain knew little about this, but in ministerial circles there was steady movement and activity in response to the information.

Mary Ryder's father was a civil servant and she remembers that he travelled to London on a daily basis, but had always kept regular hours.

> From about 1935, father spent more and more time away from home. We knew he spent long hours in his office and he often stayed in London for several days at a time. Mother, after the war, confided that she thought that he was seeing another woman. However, we did learn that he had been involved on some sort of project and because of security, he was obliged to remain at his post.

In addition to the estate at Pylewell, many other large estates, country houses and hotels were commandeered by the army. These include the Balmer Lawn Hotel at Brockenhurst, Cuffnalls at Lyndhurst and Exbury House, near Beaulieu. Within the confines of these and other properties were training establishments, military HQs, intelligence-gathering operations, convalescent homes and an entire network of logistical support units.

Thomas Knapp (a pseudonym) was a civil servant in 1939 and was 'recruited' into the Intelligence Services in 1941. After what he describes as 'having to do some fairly mundane tasks' he was given an assignment that took him to Southampton.

I travelled to Southampton by train from my office just outside London. On arrival I was met by a 'taxi', operated by my department.

You appreciate that I am not prepared to talk about every aspect of what I did; however, I can tell you some things which will not cause any problems. A chap of my age – I was twenty-one at the time – was an obvious candidate for the armed services and so I had to be given a cover, that is a reserved occupation, so that I could produce relevant papers and could rebuff any calls from members of the public that I was a draft-dodger. There were people who would call after civilians, men in particular, if you were not in uniform or your occupation wasn't obvious from what you wore. I was an Inspector for the Ministry of Food, checking various aspects of the supply and provisions of rations and so on. That was my cover.

From Southampton I went out of the city to a briefing station in a large house at the end of a gravel drive. There were a number of other people there, men and women. For several days we were given instructions and we had to learn quite a lot of information. Everyone had his or her own tasks.

By bicycle, bus and sometimes by car, my job was to travel around the Forest

Military Police stepped up security patrols in the months before D-Day. *(Author's collection)*

Routine stop-and-check of vehicles was the order of the day. *(Author's collection)*

area, going into public houses, shops, hotels and other public places to listen to people's conversations. The Forest was already home to many military personnel who were encamped, or who were training with arms and vehicles and an increasing number of installations were being requisitioned by the Army. I spent a lot of time in and around the Army and Air Force installations as they came into use. I had to report back any 'conversations' that might reasonably be considered 'unpatriotic'. There was a campaign about 'walls have ears'. Well, I was those ears if you like. I had to pick up on careless talk and that sort of thing.

Occasionally I would change with one of my women colleagues so as not to get too well known. You may think that I should have become well known and trusted in the area, but there were reasons why we had a change of personnel sometimes.

In 1944, as it got towards D-Day, I engaged in casual conversation with soldiers and airmen to find out if they would talk about the build-up and give any information away about what they thought was going on. I also had to find out if there was any dissent among the troops. That sort of thing. By this method, we could gauge the possible security risks and isolate individuals who may cause problems or breach security. I am pleased to say that we never had any reported security problems.

In between this work I was occasionally involved in debriefings of returning airmen and also, because I could speak Italian, I spent some time as a 'make-believe' Italian POW at one of the POW camps in the Forest. This was interesting, but quite challenging, although I was able to pass on some useful information to my bosses. I was also involved in the arrest of a person who was later charged with a serious offence.

After D-Day I returned to a desk job in London and only went to the Forest a couple of times between then and the end of the war. I am afraid I am not able to tell you what I was doing then or many of the other things our department was responsible for.

8

The Beaulieu Estate at War

The well-documented history of the Beaulieu estate pays fitting tribute to the men and women of the SOE, many of whom undertook their training in and around Beaulieu village and Bucklers Hard. In particular, the woods on the estate were ideal for covert training exercises, while houses were designated for specific uses. There was a German house, a French house and houses for other occupied countries. Agents could simulate the kind of situations they may find themselves in while on operations in enemy territory. They also learnt how to use small arms.

Other SOE units in London, Buckinghamshire and Hertfordshire supported the efforts of the Beaulieu station by providing equipment and additional training. Many agents flew into Occupied Europe from nearby Beaulieu Airfield, the main runway of which is partially visible today. Others flew from Tangmere,* just across the Sussex border, near Chichester.

Lord Montagu is a charismatic figure who is probably best known for his association with the family estate at Beaulieu and the world-famous Motor Museum. Lord Montagu remembers the estate being a vast military installation serving the needs of the Army and Navy as well as the SOE and the Royal Air Force. In a unique interview he tells the story from his own perspective:

The Beaulieu estate, given its position and size, was able to contribute much to the war effort. While the Special Operations Executive (SOE) agents trained on various parts of the estate, the Beaulieu river, now devoid of pleasurecraft, returned to its

* Tangmere has a superb collection of relevant period artefacts and first-hand accounts of pilots who flew the agents.

Palace House, Beaulieu. *(Author's collection)*

former use as a site for boat-building.

I suppose our first knowledge that the war had started was that we were waiting for the Chamberlain broadcast which was at 11 o'clock on 3 September. And all the family had gone to church and I was at home to hear that famous speech, and so in fact I did, and then I ran out as quickly as I could, but of course I was late at church. Rather breathlessly, I spoke down the pew, 'the war's on'.

And I remember coming out of church that day, about an hour later. There was a plane that flew overhead and everybody thought it was a German plane, and there was a great panic, but I don't think it was German.

But in 1940 I was actually sent to Canada, in July, with a lot of other children who were evacuated after the fall of France, because it was thought that Hitler was literally a few days away. And so I rather lost touch with Beaulieu during that period until I came back, and then of course I found an enormous difference.

First of all, the government had requisitioned all the major houses at Beaulieu for SOE, and they were training the secret agents who were dropped into France and other places. And that was really quite amazing because houses I used to go to and play tennis at, all the owners had gone and the houses now had been requisitioned.

The river had not a single boat on it because all the boats had to be brought and put in the garden here, so the enemy couldn't use them, if there was an invasion.

The Home Guard was very active: there were pillboxes everywhere, and of course, as time went on, more and more Army, more and more Navy came and the whole place was really a bristling Army base.

Up to D-Day, of course, it got more and more active, until the woods were full of troops, mainly from the Tyne Tees Division, the Canadian Division and the Royal Welch Fusiliers, where in fact they camped for some months before.

The river was then actually completely requisitioned by the Navy, which then requisitioned Bucklers Hard. The hotel there, the Master Builders, which is still a hotel of course, was their headquarters. In fact there's a carving on one of the mantelpieces down there, which commemorates the time they were there. And always, throughout the time of D-Day, and just before D-Day, they were making mostly torpedo boats at Bucklers Hard. And also Minka barges, which were Canadian landing craft, and they were made and assembled here out of cedarwood, I think, and then floated down, and used, for the invasion.

One very interesting man who was here during the war was Nevil Shute, who wrote the famous book *Requiem for a Wren*, which was all about Beaulieu river during the war, and of course other famous books as well. He was also involved with Exbury House, not far away from here. And he was experimenting with all sorts of funny gadgets, sort of almost James Bond type things. And I remember going down to the beach one spring and they were experimenting with controlled smoke. They were testing it with a pilot-less plane, which actually emitted smoke from its back. And I remember seeing this funny model aircraft taking off and flying round and crashing. Nevil Shute was full of great ideas, but I'm not sure any of them came to anything. But he was a great character.

And of course the whole area really was a special area and as it got to D-Day (and I went back to Eton in, I think, April 1944, just about a month or so before), I had to have a special permit to come back to my home. In fact I've still got that permit in the archives somewhere.

What sort of restrictions were

SPECIAL PERMIT

Serial No. 2352

FOR PERSONS WHOSE IDENTITY CARD DOES NOT BEAR AN ADDRESS WITHIN THE AREA, BUT WHO ARE TEMPORARILY LIVING THERE OR WHO ENTER IT FREQUENTLY FOR AN APPROVED PURPOSE

M*r* *Edward W.* .... *Montagu* (name

of *Beaulieu Manor, Elm C....* ...... *Bucks* address

whose National Registration Identity Card No is *YEEN 129 7* is hereby authorized to be treated as a resident and to

proceed to *Palace House*

.... address

within the restricted area specified in the Schedule to Direction No. 1 under Defence Regulation 3A by the General Officer Commanding in-Chief Southern Command

between *10* hours *13 August 1943* date and

.... hours *...* date for the purpose

of *residing there whilst at Palace House, Beaulieu.*

2 This permit must be carried out of doors at all times and shown on demand together with the Identity Card to any Constable or member of His Majesty's Forces on duty and must be surrendered on leaving the locality

Signature of holder *Montagu of Beaulieu*

K. Miell 1630

For the Chief Constable of

Hampshire

Date *13/8/43*

300 pads of 00 7 43 W.O.P 4523

placed upon you and your family during that time?

We really, as a family, didn't have any restrictions placed on us because we were
arranging and providing entertainment for the troops so much. I think there were
at least three dances a week in the Abbey and in time the floor was almost wrecked
because, of course, they were still in their Army boots, which really wasn't the best
footwear for use on the old floor. We entertained the officers in the house. My
sisters were at that time of marriageable age and there was a lot of courting that
went on, particularly for the Czech Air Squadron, based on Beaulieu Aerodrome.
They were flying Liberators on Coastal Command and when one of those aircraft
crashed, and one or two did on take-off, they were carrying something like
eight depth charges aboard. It really was an enormous explosion. But they were
wonderful, the Czechs, and I remember they gave me a record of the 'New World'
symphony by Dvorak, which I enjoyed playing at the time.

Did you have much involvement with the airfield and what knowledge did you have
about it?

Of course, there were two, the main Beaulieu site up on the Forest, called Beaulieu
Aerodrome, to the right of the Lymington Road as you make your way towards
Pilley. That was, of course, enormously important, and, as the Czech Squadron
left before D-Day, they then brought in the American Air Force. And, on Beaulieu
Estate itself, the aerodrome was made on Park Farm, which had Tornados, just
before D-Day. That's the Needs Ore site and it was only used for a few weeks, and
then as the Allied troops made their way into France, they set up airfields over there
and they didn't need the airfield any more. But they had a philosophy that if they
had a damaged plane coming back from France they could land anywhere when
they crossed the coast. So therefore, every 3 miles on the southern coast there was an
aerodrome they could land at, and, of course, very good planning that.
   They only laid down single summerfeld tracking, which was sort of wire, which
the grass grew through afterwards. And after the war all that was taken up and cut
up and used as fencing, I remember. There is still some of the tracking in evidence
at Park Farm.

What was the impact of the war on Beaulieu village itself and the community of
Beaulieu people?

Well, we had a tremendous number of wartime efforts, you know, Spitfire Week,
and Royal Navy, Army days, all raising money, particularly for buying aeroplanes.
I think they wanted £5,000 for a Spitfire and in the Forest as a whole we raised
a great deal of money to buy Spitfires. There was a Spitfire named New Forest,
but I think that came to a sad end and never saw much service. Everybody was
working in the war, Palace House was the headquarters for the ARP and also the

Red Cross, so it was manned day and night. Surprisingly, it was never actually requisitioned fully, because it was doing so many other things. Other houses were requisitioned for the army as well. But because the SOE was here, they kept information about the houses very secret, because it wasn't until after the war that we knew what they were doing.

We called them the 'hush hush troops' and it literally wasn't until a great sort of party at the end of the war when everybody got very drunk and celebrated that we actually knew what they were doing. Of course a lot of very famous people went through the schools here. People like Odette, Violette Szabo, and people who are now household names in the SOE. And a lot of very brave men and women went from here, never to return. And that's why in the Abbey cloisters we've got a lovely memorial to the SOE, which was particularly apt this year, when the sixtieth anniversary of the SOE coming to Beaulieu was celebrated by the Special Forces Club.

Do you recall any strange occurrences that could be attributed to the SOE? There must have been some odd things going on that later were accepted as SOE training activities.

Of course, in fact, the SOE candidates came usually in a truck which was completely covered in canvas so you couldn't see who was coming, or who was going. They were told to avoid the local population. On occasions, maybe just once or twice, I remember meeting people who were obviously pupils out in the woods on the estate, but in those days you didn't say, 'Who are you?' or ask what they were doing.

The King's headkeeper from Sandringham, who was called Nobby Clark, I think, used to teach them how to live off the land, which entailed poaching my pheasants and blowing up fish in the river, but we had to forgive them for all of that. There were one or two lapses when one saw things one really shouldn't have done.

But each of the requisitioned houses had its own functions, the German house, the French house, the finishing school house, where you were woken up in the middle of the night and interrogated. It was quite tough training here.

What was achieved by people who left here can only be told, in part, by looking through the records. Of course several quite famous people, in the main SOE executive, went back. This was a finishing school: if they didn't get through here they would be sent back to their units.

One of ways the agents left for their missions was in Lysander planes which could land and take off in very short distances, and they took off from Beaulieu Aerodrome. I think we also had people arrive at the airfield who were being 'got out' of places like Germany and Holland and France because of their importance to the Allies. Sometimes agents went by water, on fast MTBs from the Beaulieu river.

Today, the Beaulieu river is much more tranquil than it was in 1944. *(Author's collection)*

Some time ago we published some information about the SOE at Beaulieu in the war. It's amazing, of course, once this information was released, all sorts of people wrote with more information; it always happens.
How important an asset was the Beaulieu river?

. . . another contribution the river made during the war was the facilities provided for building parts of the Mulberry Harbour. They first of all built an enormous great concrete floating dock and everybody thought it was going to sink – nobody had thought about making a boat out of concrete. It didn't sink, it floated, and parts of it are still in use, I think, up in Norway. But also, after that construction was built, they made quite a lot of the other component parts for the Mulberry

Harbour, and that went on right through till after D-Day. So the river did, one way and another, make a great contribution. And being a privately owned river, of course, we could keep it extremely secure.

What was life like at Beaulieu in the weeks before D-Day?

Just before D-Day Beaulieu literally became an armed camp. You see you had to have your special permit to get back in to the estate. The woods were full of troops, the river full of boats. The Solent was full of boats too. Then of course they delayed D-Day by twenty-four hours because of the weather. All the troops on the landing craft had fortty-eight-hour packs of food, and they were told to throw overboard their original pack in order get to the new forty-eight-hour packs. So we had the most wonderful time the next few weeks, with all this food that had been washed up on the beach, some of it we'd never seen before, and some we had not seen for ages, like butter, and so on. That was a bonus result of delaying D-Day for twenty-four hours.

And of course we, as young men in those days, were required to do war work, and I worked on a farm, getting the harvest, stooking the corn, and making haystacks and so on.

Did you realise that D-Day was actually happening?

You see the problem was that I was on school holidays in April 1944 and then went back to Eton at the end of that month, so I was at school when D-Day actually happened. Before I went away it was quite obvious that something of great importance was going to happen with this enormous build-up going on. My stepfather was Chief of Staff down at Weymouth and he was dealing with the planning and implementation of the invasion. He was unable to tell us anything because of the very high security. But we knew it was about to happen and one was just waiting for the moment when one heard from the BBC that it had happened.

What was it like when you returned and suddenly there was nothing going on – it had all happened, everyone was the other side of the Channel? Was it an interesting time, an exciting time, a nervous time?

Even after D-Day there was actually a tremendous amount still going on, because they were making the landing craft still and the Minka barges because, after all, they were being used in the invasion, the Upper Rhine and so on. I have to say that there weren't quite so many people around. There were certain sighs of relief when we were allowed to put the boats back on the river and go sailing. The war was still on and I don't think one was relieved of that feeling really until VE Day. Really everything came right on VE Day. All the SOE houses were very soon derequisitioned. Everybody knew what they were doing and things got back to normal quite soon I think.

The physical remains of the war include the pillboxes, one of which is right in the centre of the village, and there is the strongpoint too which you can still see by the bridge. The bridge itself was strengthened to take the tanks and heavy military vehicles and it is marked with a plate saying 1943. There are still some of the old rafters where the barges were built. Interestingly, when they were putting down the new timbers, they came across the old timbers that were used in the eighteenth century to build the Bucklers Hard ships. They'd been in the mud all that time and were so hard they could hardly get a nail in them and so they built the new one on top. So it's rather historically interesting that the structures used for previous wars were used again in the Second World War.

I must confess that as a teenager war was quite exciting and I always dreamed of being a Spitfire pilot. In fact I went into the Army in the end, but I deeply loved the Spitfire and, of course, a lot of them were made not far from here over in Eastleigh so one saw quite a lot of them. Yes, for me the war was exciting and at that age one grew used to having a completely different life, one hitchhiked to places for example and people would stop and give you a lift and you did not fear being attacked or robbed. One didn't have cars like young people do today. I had driving lessons in the war, it sounds rather strange, but the government did allow a certain amount of petrol to be used for driving lessons and I used to bicycle all the way from here to Hythe, go on the ferry, bicycle into Southampton and have a short lesson, driving round the Southampton streets.

Today here at Beaulieu the visitor will see the plaque to the SOE – there are

Boat trips along the Beaulieu river pass the sites of Second World War boat-building and the remnants of parts of a Mulberry Harbour. *(Author's collection)*

some photographs of wartime interest and one can see the pillboxes and so on. We have the museum at Bucklers Hard and there are many references to the Beaulieu river at war and there is evidence of the airfield up on the road to Lymington.

9

Exbury in Military Service

At Exbury, the Rothschild family estate (renamed Her Majesty's Stone Frigate *Mastodon*), Naval Intelligence was busy collecting vital data. Over 1,000 naval personnel were stationed here in massed ranks of Nissen huts which were built right across the site. More naval personnel were employed on the nearby Beaulieu river. King George VI and Winston Churchill were among the many distinguished visitors who witnessed the contribution made by staff at *Mastodon*. Just across the estate, at Inchmery House, Free French and Polish commandos were in training for their part in the intelligence war.

On 6 June 1997 *Mastodon*'s original white ensign was handed over to the

Edmund de Rothschild passes the flag to the Commanding Officer of HMS *King Alfred*, 6 June 1997.
(Author's collection)

commanding officer of HMS *King Alfred* at a ceremony in the grounds of Exbury House. Edmund de Rothschild, himself a former intelligence officer, and former members of the Intelligence staff were present on this very emotional occasion.

After the Remembrance Sunday service in 2000, a tree was planted in the grounds of the Exbury estate. Carved in stone from nearby Beaulieu Abbey, a small memorial was dedicated to all those who served at the site during the war years.

Exbury Gardens is open to the public during the summer months. Visitors can stroll in the footsteps of the servicemen and women who were based here during the war; however, unlike that wartime generation, the visitor today has time to enjoy the scenery. Those who worked at Mastoden had little time to enjoy the glorious grounds and wonderful views.

The family home of Edmund de Rothschild is situated on the shores of the Solent and adjacent to the Beaulieu river. The grounds and gardens of the house are world famous for the variety of rhododendrons which grow there.

Mr de Rothschild was asked when he first learned that his family home was due to be requisitioned by the army.

Well it started, actually, before my father died in January 1942. But before that the

Edmund de Rothschild. *(Author's collection)*

The imposing façade of Exbury House overlooking the Solent. *(Author's collection)*

house had been emptied of most of its really valuable contents because we were prepared for the bombing of Southampton. I was released from the Army for a month and a half to start paying off some of the death duties, selling the various things, and then I rejoined my regiment. Now I'd been commissioned actually, in the third generation in the Royal Bucks Yeomanry.

Suddenly, in May, the colonel sent for me. We were up in Scotland and he said 'Eddie, the Admiralty want you down at Exbury House, so here's a rail pass and I think that we will be gone overseas by the time you come back. You will have to make your own way. There's a train leaving Glasgow tonight, it's a sealed train and it will stop just outside London and that's where you get off.'

So that's what I did and I made my way down to Exbury and I met the Admiralty man. He said that I had to remove all my stuff from the house in just forty-eight hours!

Well, I was very strong in those days and I started moving the bits of furniture out that were still left here. In fact, there was a lot left and the villagers helped and the farm labourers helped out too. I then went back and rejoined my regiment and came back to Exbury in 1946, having gone to Algeria and Tunisia and then from the bottom to the top of Italy.

So I only knew secondhand what was happening at Exbury. But the Admiralty kept the house on till after the war, as late as 1955 in fact. The gamekeeper, William Rachell, wrote me a letter every week, telling me about the state of the harvest, and the number of partridges there were, or about the pheasants or the fine weather or the gardens, but he never mentioned anything about who was occupying the house, or anything like that.

In fact, Exbury became one of the local centres for the planning for D-Day.

About 17 miles to the north-west of Exbury is Breamore House, and that was, for a very short time, General George Patton's headquarters. And 17 miles to the south-east was General Eisenhower's headquarters at Southwick House (today known as HMS *Dryad*), and 17 miles to the north was Bernard Montgomery's headquarters. On the Beaulieu river, which is at the bottom of the garden, the landing craft of various sizes were tested out and finally used for the invasion of Normandy in 1944, D-Day. There is in fact a wreck of a small naval craft still in the mud to this day.

And the whole of the Solent was filled with landing craft. Now the King, George VI, particularly asked the War Department that if it was possible, that no guns and tanks should be parked in the garden at Exbury because of the rare species of some of our plants and so on. Just before D-Day, as everyone knows, the whole of this area of the New Forest was filled with tanks and guns and everything else, but not, thankfully, in the garden here at Exbury.

There is still today a walk in the gardens down to Gilbury Pier at the Beaulieu river. In those days you could almost cross the river, as Nevil Shute in his book *Requiem for a Wren* points out, by walking from one Tank Landing Craft (TLC) to another.

And then the whole of Lepe, just along the shore here, was filled with craft – and from Lepe foreshore, of course, one part of the Pluto oil pipeline started.

Now, one of the things that happened here which is, perhaps, apocryphal, is when the powers that be and the military planners realised that it was very difficult, after the problems at Dieppe, to capture a port in northern France. Further attempts to capture ports would result in tremendous casualties and the whole operation would be very difficult. There was subsequently a major meeting of the military engineers and this took place in the gardens here under the shade of a large tree that was just behind what we call the Captain's Cottage. They decided, yes, they could find a solution to the problem and the first trials and the first idea was going to be started and tested at Bucklers Hard.

Now at the end of this top level meeting or conference, call it what you will, which took place on a very hot July day, someone asked, 'Now what shall we call it?' A young naval officer piped up and said, 'Well as you have been working under the shade of a mulberry tree why don't we simply call it, Mulberry Harbour?' So Exbury really got that claim for fame that the Mulberry Harbour, which of course now is a sort of legend, began here in the grounds. I don't think that is widely realised.

Mr de Rothschild was asked where he and the family lived during this time.

The family lived in the village. My father had a laundry and there was a flat in the laundry so we moved to that flat. My mother was then able to move in with us all.

I made an agreement with the Admiralty that the villagers of Exbury would not be moved and so everything was kept very much as it was. However, the houses were filled with Wrens who were billeted everywhere. Also, there were twenty-three Nissen huts and there were 1,300 naval officers and ratings. And they had their mess in the drawing-room of Exbury House and I think they were very well looked after.

A chap by the name of Captain Swinley was one of the commanders here and he was a very pugnacious man. He was actually very disappointed that he hadn't got the command of any ships. HMS *Mastodon*, which is what we were called, was a stone frigate. To us Swinley was an extraordinary person. He kept some pigs, he grew some vegetables and he was a misogynist.

I recall that the king come to pay a visit on one occasion. Captain Swinley said to the Wrens billeted all about, 'I am sorry ladies, there is not enough room on the lawn for you all to be here when the King visits. However, you may lie in the ha-ha, which is at the bottom of the lawn, or if you wish, you may go into the shrubbery and watch from there.'

Now, the King didn't like walking through the ranks very much, but he did walk to the rear rank of men at the back of the lawn. To his surprise he spotted, in the ha-ha, a whole lot of heads – and hatbands – with HMS *Mastodon* on the cap. Yes, it was the Wrens who were 'hidden' at the request of Swinley.

Now Swinley knew that my father had taken King George VI round the garden when he was Duke of York, with the Duchess, later the Queen Mother. The gardens were in flower and he got hold of the agent, called Mr Hare, who was not well enough to go to the war and he made him go round with his writer who had to take the names of the different flowers. And the King replied to Captain Swinley who had just asked him, 'Would you like me, Your Majesty, to go round the grounds and the gardens with you? Shall I shall accompany you?' And the King said bluntly, 'No!'

Then the King walked on his own down the path to the pond where the azaleas were out and he sat there for twenty minutes thinking what his men were going to go through when they were embroiled in the D-Day landings.

Well, as you know there was a storm, but just before the storm a German plane did succeed in coming through, and although in *Requiem for a Wren* it was supposed to have been shot down by one of the Wrens, that's just not the case. It was actually shot down by one of our own Typhoon aircraft. And it landed in the park, farther over the estate in a muddy field.

One of the crew was just alive. The dentist, who now lives in Australia and whom I have contacted, well, he tried to get the mud out of the nostrils and the mouth and the throat of this one person who could possibly have been alive out of the many people who were in the craft. Unfortunately he failed and the local policeman had the task of dealing with the incident.

Now a book is being written about them or studies are being made, and there is a person doing some research, because they have contacted the relatives of those that were shot down and have shown them where they are buried. And they're now buried properly and with proper honours. We don't know, nobody knows, whether they were actually seeking asylum or were trying to take photographs. Because the person who was the aviator, I'll call him that even though he was a pretty poor aviator, who landed in the park, had all the papers, perhaps to take them somewhere so that they could be looked at properly. As the plane turned left, going over the trees, he crashed, they were killed and all the documentation was burnt. That was one of the stories of the house.

The other story was, when Captain Swinley sent for the very old caretaker who looked after the two rooms that were not taken over by the military. The rooms were where the furniture was just piled up. Swinley sent for the caretaker and said, 'I think we ought to open Captain Rothschild's cellar, because my men are going to suffer great danger.' And Mr Whist drew himself up and said, 'My Captain, Captain Rothschild has been in much greater danger many more years than any of your people.' With that Whist was given a 'hot line' to the Admiralty and within an hour, the man from the Admiralty came out and that was the end of Mr Swinley. You see it seems he had just gone too far anyway, but trying to gain access to the wine in the cellar on the pretence of saving his men was too much.

But it didn't quite end there because when Swinley's son came to see me I took him on at the bank for a short time as a personnel officer. So that is the tale of Captain Swinley.

Then after 1944 and D-Day, at the beginning of 1945, the house became HMS *King Alfred*, and after that HMS *Hawk*. Anyway, as it was so important to have an area of land available on the marshes, where they could practise assault landings and keep the commandos there, they then kept the house until 1955, because Montgomery was very frightened about the Russians and the Cold War. So it was only in 1955 that the house, empty, came back into our possession.

Anyway, back to the time of the Second World War. Later we lived at a house called Inchmery, down the road, where there had been commandos. Now, there had to be very, very important security and Miriam Lane, as Miriam Rothschild, that is Lord Rothschild's aunt, the present Lord Rothschild's aunt, fell in love with a Hungarian called Lanie. He changed his name to Lane and he was one of these irregular types working for an Intelligence department. He learnt the Welsh language so that if he was captured while on a mission, he would speak in Welsh and would be able to talk knowledgeably about the town that he had adopted as his home town: a Welsh town where he got to know everybody.

One of his tasks was to go across the Channel to test the mines before the landings. On the last day of tests, having as usual left from Inchmery House, which is here on the estate, he was captured.

He was taken before Rommel, and Rommel was very polite to him and said to him, now I have had orders from Hitler to kill saboteurs like you, but as you have been so brave I am going to send you to a PoW camp. And he then offered him tea and then George Lane asked Rommel some questions. Rommel said, what's a good Aryan boy like you fighting against us for when you should be fighting against the Russians?

Anyway, then the Gestapo questioned him, which wasn't so pleasant, and he was taken then to the PoW camp where he was treated as a spy among them. As Lane had left Rommel's headquarters in Normandy, he had in fact noted that there was a right-hand turn after so many seconds and a left-hand turn and so on and he was able to get these details passed to the RAF. They were then able to pinpoint the castle in which Rommel was situated. That's how Rommel was actually wounded by an aeroplane when he left the hideout. This is where Von Runstedt was, it was his headquarters. And that's quite a story.

Earlier, I was telling you about the wines. The wines were left intact and luckily the cellar was not broken into.

Now we've got an Exbury Veterans' Association and some of the people who come to the house today used to walk in the gardens all those years ago, at all times of the year. Perhaps not so much in winter, because although the tracery of the trees is quite beautiful the wind is usually blowing very hard and the trees are bowing to a storm. But nevertheless, they found an aura of peace in the gardens before they were going into action.

So a great many people passed through Exbury House in the times before the Normandy landings. Those service personnel who came after, the ones who had trained here also, were allowed to join the Veterans. Now the Exbury Veterans' Association is over 100 members strong and it is organised by a very good man called Clive Leicester.

Moving on, we think we know where the hospital stood, where the guardroom was and where the dentist had his little dentist's chair, and that is quite interesting. As I said, there were twenty-three Nissen huts and after all the events of war we had to take these huts down. But the Navy were extremely good because when I came back to the house the damage that was done was literally very, very minimal and I suppose because they had all been rather senior officers it should have been minimal!

Other major people who came to see the house included Naval Admiral Sir Bertram Ramsey, HM the King, who came twice, and Montgomery – but I never found out from him. I didn't know he knew the house, and I don't think he actually paid a visit here during the time that the planning was done for different parts of the Normandy landings.

Winston Churchill wanted to visit again because he had been here before the war. He had put his hand to trying to paint a picture of the azaleas at the pond, but he just gave up saying that it was far too difficult. I believe he even tore up his canvas. Whether he came on after we don't know, but he wanted to go with the landings and witness them. He was asked not to and prevented by all the generals and admirals. He still insisted on going and finally it went to higher authority and the King forbade him to go.

Churchill took an apartment in Portsmouth and watched the assault landings going from there. The King, it is thought, actually came down and went down to the pier and saw it, but that's not been confirmed.

Mr de Rothschild was asked about security on the estate during the war years.

Well, security was very tight; however, it's quite extraordinary how security can be broken in the most odd ways. George Lane, whom I mentioned earlier, had married Miriam Rothschild. Ordinarily, they both loved sending and receiving letters, but at one time when he was here George wrote to Miriam, 'I can't write to you. I'm afraid I can't tell you where I am.'

However, two days later, George received a reply from Miriam. 'I will meet you in Exbury church at 12 o'clock.' George's letter had been posted here at the local post office and sure enough on the envelope was stamped 'Exbury', so she knew where he was. So that was the only break in security that there was, that we know of anyway. The clerk responsible for the mail had overlooked the obvious postmark, which I don't believe should have been on the envelope anyway.

On another aspect of security, there were a lot of troops guarding the more sensitive areas, but they did not know what they were guarding.

When the war in Europe ended, how soon was the Estate demobilised and what was it like after that?

The house was demobilised in 1955; however, we were allowed back before that time. It was peace time, 1946, when I came back. I looked to see what was there and by then the furniture was being sold to pay the death duties of up to 75 per cent. So that was really my first job, to deal with that and then I had to enter the bank, the family bank. At Exbury we were farming and I went round the garden and thought to myself, well, as the gardens were only put in at £1 into the probate it's not difficult to pay out the fifteen shillings death duty.

We decided to clean the house and we had six men in to help with this. We worked thoroughly and then finally in the 1960s we opened to the public for the first time. We had such a mass of people wanting to see the gardens that the whole of the road almost up to Dibden Purlieu was clogged with cars. Not many people had cars in those days so you can imagine this was quite something.

And then, after the great storm in recent years, we had 7,000 visitors in one day to see the damage done. Luckily, we got over that because, when I came down and saw my head gardener, there was one tree over the plant centre and I said to him 'We'll have that tree down. The crop garden is undamaged, the azalea walk is undamaged and there are a lot of trees left, we'll make a new garden.'

We started rebuilding the garden and it's quite astonishing how quickly regeneration has taken place. New oaks have sprung up from acorns that fell and all sorts of other trees did survive, or from the roots, they were cut down and they have come up from the roots which happens. So people have different times of the year that they want to come. For example, the first flower to come out is called *hamamelis mollis*, which is witchhazel, and it's the basis of Pond's extract of cold cream.

Then the very early rhododendrons, they are not very beautiful. Then the daffodils or rhododendrons, evergreen azaleas or rhododendrons, deciduous azaleas and then the late flowering rhododendrons. Now we've planted up all sorts of different shrubs and flowers and we hope that people come just to enjoy the peace and rest in a garden – just as those servicemen and women did.

Recently a 'special' tree planting ceremony took place in the grounds of Exbury House. Mr de Rothschild describes this occasion.

The veterans wanted to have a special service and so for the 11th of November they asked me to plant a tree. There is a commemorative plaque for all those that fell during the landings, or who passed through the house and died subsequently. The veterans have also given us a very fine bench so that people can sit and see the flagpole.

Now on the 50th anniversary of D-Day there were special events that took place all over the country. I helped very much with regard to 'Hampshire Remembers D-Day' and with the deputy lieutenant and one of the generals, we got together about 10,000 people here and the Duke of Edinburgh came down in a helicopter and Southampton Water was filled with people. It rained the day before and it rained the day after, but on the day itself it was fine, but very muddy. No tanks or guns were able to come in so soggy was the ground.

And I asked permission that on 6 June, the actual day when the Wrens had gone down to wave good-bye to the sailors and the troops leaving for Normandy, that we could fly the white ensign from our flagpole. I asked the Admiralty whether we could, and back came the answer 'no way'. Then I asked the Ministry of Defence and they said 'Oh no, sorry no. Write to higher authority,' which I subsequently did.

Back came the answer, 'Her Majesty has been graciously pleased to grant you the sole and exceptional privilege of flying the white ensign for one day to

commemorate those gallant men and women who passed through Exbury House in
the Second World War.'

10

Waterside's War

Waterside is on the eastern edge of the Forest and covers an area south
of Totton to Calshot at the mouth of Southampton Water. All Saints'
church in Fawley has, like all the other churches in the Forest, served the

Home Secretary Herbert Morrison inspects Fire Service Overseas Contingent at Totton. *(Hampshire Fire
& Rescue Service)*

community through both wars. Significantly, it has provided a place of worship and comfort to the men and women who served on the former RAF Calshot base nearby.

Waterside contributed much to the war effort. Eling Tide Mill, near Totton, for example, supplied water to the nearby Fawley refinery which in turn supplied fuel via PLUTO to the shores of France. Eight marines were assigned the task of guarding Eling although they all complained that they wanted to see more action than Eling could ever provide!

❖   ❖   ❖

May Belbin (née Yearsley) lived in Southampton, but just a couple of days before the outbreak of war she moved to Totton. She later joined the National Fire Service and served at Testwood.

I was working in domestic service for several people in the Southampton area. I was very lucky because I was often recommended for job opportunities. I had my son Stan to take care of, so money was always handy, and I needed somewhere to work where accommodation was available. We moved to our present address to be in service for a chap who invited me to work for him and he was very kind and was

May Belbin joins the NFS.
(*May Belbin*)

May and the team at Testwood. (*May Belbin*)

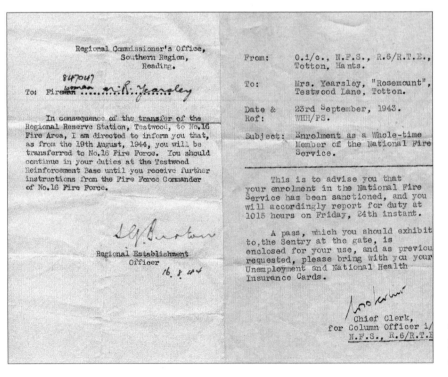

Regional Commissioner's Office,
Southern Region,
Reading.

847047

To: Fireman .... M.R. Yearsley

In consequence of the transfer of the
Regional Reserve Station, Testwood, to No.16
Fire Area, I am directed to inform you that,
as from the 19th August, 1944, you will be
transferred to No.16 Fire Force. You should
continue in your duties at the Testwood
Reinforcement Base until you receive further
instructions from the Fire Force Commander
of No.16 Fire Force.

Regional Establishment
Officer
16.8.44

From: O.i/c., N.F.S., R.6/R.T.E.,
Totton, Hants.

To: Mrs. Yearsley, "Rosemount",
Testwood Lane, Totton.

Date & 23rd September, 1943.
Ref: WHH/PS.

Subject: Enrolment as a Whole-time
Member of the National Fire
Service.

This is to advise you that
your enrolment in the National Fire
Service has been sanctioned, and you
will accordingly report for duty at
1015 hours on Friday, 24th instant.

A pass, which you should exhibit
to the Sentry at the gate, is
enclosed for your use, and as previou
requested, please bring with you your
Unemployment and National Health
Insurance Cards.

Chief Clerk,
for Column Officer i/
N.F.S., R.6/R.T.E

The paperwork was
kept simple in those
days. (*May Belbin*)

An NFS display at Testwood, *c.* 1943. (*Hampshire Fire & Rescue Service*)

very fond of Stan. We were always in a family atmosphere and we were treated no different to the rest of the family, you know we were not made to feel unwelcome.

I think we moved here on 1 September 1939 and there were open fields in front of the house and it was great for the children and I was happy in my work. After the war had started a friend asked me if I would like to join the fire service who were in real need of people. I wasn't sure what it was all about but I went for the interview and was sent for a medical. It was very thorough and a little later a dispatch rider called and gave me a note to say that I had been accepted. I was to work in the domestic side of the service, looking after the meals for the men at Testwood, which was a main centre for the National Fire Service.

I hadn't done cooking on a large scale but I soon got the hang of it and the men said how good my cooking was. The chef was a real stickler. He would keep us on our toes all the time and if we seemed to be enjoying ourselves he would take a very dim view of it. When some of the men made comments about us, you know, flattering comments, he would get quite cross. He used to enjoy his drink too so it was best to keep out of his way as much as possible. They were a good bunch of people at Testwood. The men used to come for a break from fire

NATIONAL FIRE SERVICE   NO.6 FIRE REGION HEADQUARTERS

NOTICE OF DISCHARGE - WHOLE-TIME PERSONNEL

To: 847047 Firewoman Yearsley.

Address: Rose Mount, Testwood Lane,

             Totton, Hants.

    Notice is hereby given to you that under Regulation 7(4) of the
National Fire Service (General) Regulations, 1944, you are hereby
discharged from the National Fire Service.

    This Notice takes effect at midnight on   28th March, 1946.

                              Regional Establishments Officer
                        By direction of Chief Regional Fire Officer

Date: 21st March, 1946.

NOTE: A separate communication will be addressed to you
         regarding the amount of post-war credit accrued.

    M.461/46.

The discharge notice arrives. (*May Belbin*)

fighting in the cities. They would stay a few days, then go back and more would
take their place.

   Later we had the Canadian fire fighters. They were wonderful, very fit and very
smooth tongued. We had good times with all the chaps who stayed at Testwood.
Apart from chef, all the staff were very nice. Later I moved up to Stoney Cross
airfield to the fire service workshops and did catering there. It was quite a way out
so we had a coach to take us backwards and forwards.

Hythe and Dibden seen from a German reconnaissance aircraft. Note Hythe Pier in the foreground and fields (top left) with 'criss-cross' barriers to prevent enemy aircraft from landing. *(Forestry Commission)*

The ancient parish of Fawley, which stretches out across the southern tip of Waterside, parallel to Southampton Water, takes in Hythe,* Fawley and Holbury and Blackfield, right down to Lepe, famous for its association with the PLUTO pipeline and the launch of the Mulberry Harbours. It used to include Exbury as

---

*Various craft, including MTBs and gunboats, were built at Hythe.

Fireboats on
Southampton Water,
c. 1943. *(Hampshire Fire
& Rescue Service)*

well, but in the mid-1800s both Hythe and Exbury were removed and the parish now covers only the area from the Hardley roundabout down to the sea.

All Saints' church has had connections with the Armed Forces since the very early days of Calshot, when the Royal Flying Corps established an important base. In the grounds of All Saints' is a scattering of First World War graves, and there is a connection between the parish and T.E. Lawrence (Lawrence of Arabia) who worked at Langley for a time, although he often visited Hythe and other places on Waterside. The church also has other aviation connections, particularly with some of the graves of the early flyers, those trying to break the air speed record in the years after the First World War and in the early 1920s. Probably the best known of these is Flight Lieutenant Kincaid, who died on 12 March 1928, and is buried in All Saints' churchyard.

The Reverend Gary Philbrick was the parish priest at Fawley until 1999, before moving to a new ministry in Southampton. He takes a great deal of interest in local history, finding time during his other more godly duties to study books on the subject.

How did the Second World War affect the church and the life of the community?

I suppose the biggest physical impact on the church was a bomb which was dropped in November 1940. All Saints' church was the second of the churches in the Waterside area to be bombed. The roof fell in and a large board was subsequently fitted across the church, almost as a substitute roof. Quite a few people have told me that they had either the last wedding before the bomb or the first one afterwards. Judging by this, there must have been quite a lot of first weddings after the bomb! The church was gradually repaired over the next few years up until 1954, when it was fully restored back to its former glory.

Outside, in the churchyard, there are a number of war graves from the Second World War, including those of the whole crew of a Hampden plane which went down. They were all buried together here. There were quite a lot of German war graves as well. However, at some time in the 1960s they were taken to the German War Cemetery in Cannock Chase, Staffordshire. They were reinterred there, so that all the German war graves could be together.

By the way, the Hampden bomber which went down had the number B5392 and was from 408 Squadron. It met its end as it returned from Cherbourg in the small hours of 15 December 1941. And this is the way it's recorded: 'This aircraft crashed at New Farm at Longdown, near Christchurch and was entirely burnt out'. Can I just say that we have a Longdown quite near here, near Totton, and there is some confusion as to whether it was locally that the aircraft crashed? That would make sense if the crew were buried here. Anyway, the records continue: 'only three bodies were recovered from the debris and are so far unidentifiable. The fourth member of the crew has not yet been recovered and instructions were issued that a communal burial should take place. Two bodies were eventually identified and all four were buried at RAF Calshot.' In fact they are buried in the churchyard at All Saints' church, Fawley – again a bit of confusion and different from what was recorded at the time.*

One of the fathers asked if he could see the remains of his son, and perhaps understandably that request was refused. And so the four men that we have still resting here today are Sergeant Stirling, Sergeant Tomlin, Sergeant Williams and Sergeant Gibson.

All Saints' church today is very active within the community it serves. In fact there are all sorts of things going on, in all the churches in this parish. As we look to the future we are also very conscious of the past, because the past is still very much alive and with us. The church is becoming established as a place where people can come and remember those who died either in the war, or in aircraft accidents over the last years. There is a collection of flags of some of the Allied nations that were involved in the Second World War and these are displayed within the church. It is hoped that in time that there will be an exhibition in the church as well, which will explain something of the history of this area and in particular of the contacts with wartime airfields in the New Forest. There is also of course the annual Remembrance Service in November, which is very well attended here by both young and old. I hope this practice will continue for many years into the future as well. So it's a mixture really of both looking to the future and being alive and active and a part of the community now, but also remembering the past.

Calshot, situated on the spit at the entrance to Southampton Water, is, today, a popular leisure complex and a viewpoint for watching the ships entering and leaving port. It is possibly the oldest military site anywhere in the Forest with a history spanning several centuries, although, without doubt, it is the connection with seaplanes that has given Calshot such a legendary reputation.

One of the most intriguing aspects of Calshot's wartime history is its use as a base for Heinkel He115 floatplanes. Norwegian pilots flew a number of these enemy

Calshot had been a military site for many generations. It is now a major leisure complex. *(Author's collection)*

* There is some doubt as to the contents of the graves. It is rumoured that at least one grave contains a coffin full of bricks and the body it should contain is interred elsewhere.

planes to England and at least one was subsequently pressed into service by British Intelligence. One can only speculate as to exactly what use these machines were put because such was the nature of the missions that the official records will not be released until 2010.

We do know that one of the Heinkels completed thirty-eight missions into enemy territory. We also know that the two floats on the plane were fitted with electric motors so that when the main engines were cut, the plane could manoeuvre quietly through the water. The floats were also hollowed out and fitted with seats and a small protective glass shield. One agent would sit in each float, making it easier for transfer to a boat or the shore.

John Iverach, a Canadian, was the aircraft's navigator. He talked very little about the missions, but he was able to reveal that every time a mission was imminent, the Royal Air Force was on standby to provide an escort aircraft. On one occasion Spitfires piloted by Polish airmen attacked the Heinkel as it returned to friendly skies over the Channel. They had not received information telling them that

A forest camp near Waterside. Fire cover was provided by the NFS during the build-up to D-Day. *(Hampshire Fire & Rescue Service)*

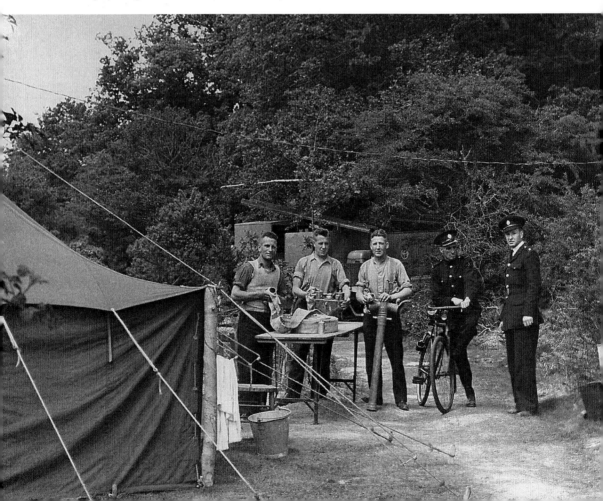

the aircraft was 'one of ours'. The aircraft was downed in the Channel and was eventually towed back to Calshot. None of the crew was hurt.

11

Stoney Cross: Memories of a Teenager

North of the main A31 trunk road, which effectively splits the Forest in half, is Canada Cross. During the war the Canadians who were stationed in the area regularly gathered on this site. This was a special place where church services were held for all denominations in the build-up to D-Day, and today the fallen are still remembered by veteran families who gather here for commemorative events. For tourists and visitors to the Forest who happen to come across the site by chance, Canada Cross is a poignant reminder of the realities of war.

Conceived as a secret airfield, Stoney Cross, adjacent to the A31, was originally built on 500 acres of heavily wooded and open forest land between Jaynesmoor plain and Milkham enclosure. Aircraft were to be stored in camouflaged hides and the site was to be without all the usual, highly visible airfield facilities. However, the decision was subsequently taken to change the use to an advance base for bombers and fighters – including Mustangs and Liberators – and so work commenced in early 1942 to achieve this plan. The station became operational in autumn 1943, by which time it had expanded to nearly double its size, at 898 acres.

In recent times much of the remaining airfield road network has been dug up. Remnants of the

People regularly visit Canada Cross to lay flowers in memory of the Canadians based in the Forest. *(Author's collection)*

Stoney Cross airfield water tower, 2004. *(Author's collection)*

site can still be seen, however. The water tower is clearly visible due east of the main runway, which itself is imprinted alongside the road from Fritham. To the side of the road and a few hundred paces from the road are the remains of some of

The imprint of Stoney Cross can still be seen from the air. *(Author's collection)*

the runway lights, at least one of which retains part of its glass dome, and broken pieces of the concrete runway are scattered liberally around the area. The width of the runway is massive even by today's standards. The imprint of a second runway is also visible, running north-east from the eastern edge of the main runway.

Harold Sturgess was a Royal Engineer. He had to be very versatile in his role, which took him to many of the military installations in the Forest. He particularly remembers Stoney Cross because one of his many tasks involved explosives. His job was to replace explosives under the runway. In case of landings by the enemy, the runways were to be blown up so that they could not be immediately operational. Harold explains:

Every so many months the explosives needed replacing and we used to clear the MacNaughton tubing under the runway of the old stuff and replace it with new explosive material. It was a special type of explosive, I can't remember the name. We then used to take the old live stuff on a lorry to a field in Chandlers Ford and blow it all up. The lorry was a real boneshaker; there was always a chance the material would explode. It wasn't like all the sophisticated explosives they have today.

❖   ❖   ❖

Marjorie Mathew still lives in the New Forest, not far from Stoney Cross, where she spent time as a teenager during the war. Her home overlooks what she calls 'my beloved New Forest' and in her retirement years she is able to enjoy the peace and tranquillity of long walks across the heathland. From the war years she remembers the military training exercises and, later, the massive build-up to D-Day. As she says herself, 'I was young enough to be still impressionable, but old enough to understand what was going on'. Her parents ran a tea-room, Dick Turpin's Cottage, situated just beyond what is now a roadside café and motel at Stoney Cross, on the A31, westbound as it leaves the M27 motorway.

Marjorie was working in Southampton at the outbreak of war, but Southampton was blitzed:

My office was no more, it was just a pile of rubble . . . and so I had to look around and try to get a job fairly quickly, because of course I had to get the money coming in to pay my way. The Ministry of Food had set up an organisation in Lyndhurst – that's the organisation that distributed the ration books – so I applied for a job there. Actually I was intending that it should just be a temporary job; however, before long it became a reserved occupation, so I couldn't get away after all. In fact, I was there in Lyndhurst for the whole war. I didn't mind too much because

One of Southampton's fleet of fire service vehicles. *(Hampshire Fire & Rescue Service)*

the office was much closer to home than having to travel into what seemed a very dangerous Southampton.

Did the invasion of the Forest by military personnel affect your routine or daily life to any degree?

Well, when later on in the war the aerodrome at Stoney Cross was built, of course it brought a nice lot of business to my parents at the tea-room. We served coffee and lunches and afternoon teas and so on. Having the airfield so close by was really quite a relief for my parents, because when the war first broke out business dropped away completely because people were simply too scared to come out or travel far from their homes. However, once the aerodrome was completed and all the service personnel were there, well, we had our tea-room crammed with all the airmen who came down here off from Stoney Cross.

Well, we started off with the bomber lads, yes, I think they were here first of all, and then we had in succession quite a variety of nationalities. Sometimes we had the maroon berets, we then had quite a few of the lads, so far from home, they had 'Canada' emblazoned on their shoulder patches. Of course we can't forget that we had the British fighter boys. We also had the Women's Auxiliary Air Force stationed around here, and I always remember that there was quite a nice little trio of WAAFs. I don't know whether they had arranged it thus, but one of the girls was blonde, one girl was brunette and one girl was a lovely redhead. They always used to come in regularly and every time they always asked for Welsh rarebit. They obviously had a great liking for this particular dish and who knows, perhaps it reminded them of home, a comfort food perhaps. Then of course, later on, we ended up with the American Air Force boys and once the Americans came there was a noticeable change. They played baseball on the area of green opposite our tea-room. Over the road and down in the woods opposite was what they called their PX, which I think was the equivalent to our NAAFI canteen. I remember that there, they sold all sorts of wonderful things like 'candy bars', which we called chocolate. They really didn't seem to lack anything. Then, of course, not too much longer after the Americans came, it was perhaps a year or maybe less than that, suddenly the war in Europe was over.

I have to say that is one of the most vivid memories I have of my life, during the war at the tea-room.

The tea-room at Dick Turpin's Cottage had a door that opened straight into it. And in the summertime my parents used to leave that door open to let the sunshine come in, and, roaming in the Forest then, as now, there were a lot of Forest ponies just grazing and lazily going about their business. In the summertime these were rounded up into groups of mares, by the stallions, which were put out into the Forest from April to September to perform their fatherly duties. They were rather bad-tempered horses actually, I remember. But the horse in question was Jonathan, and he was somebody's old pet who had been put out to end his days in peace. Of course, because Jonathan's manhood had been taken away from him in his youth, the stallions disliked him intensely. However, Jonnie, as we called him, didn't mind at all because he loved human beings and they loved him. He used to stand with his nose just over the threshold of the open door on a summer's day and he had his nose patted and he was given little bits of buttered scone and titbits like that. One day, he was standing over the doorstep, when around the corner of the house came a stallion. Now, I don't know whether his love life had been soured and made him rather bad-tempered but at any rate, he saw Jonnie's plump rump protruding from the door, and he bit it very hard indeed. Jonnie gave a scream of pain and indignation and shot straight forward into the tea-room and up between all the tables that were laid up for tea. When he reached the end of the tea-room, he spent a penny that really should have warranted an entry in the *Guinness Book of Records*!

Well, there stood Jonnie in the middle of his home-made lake, quivering with fright. The customers, who were all townies and completely unused to these rural romps, stood on their chairs and screamed in disbelief. And my parents had the awful task of backing this frightened horse out and then mopping up what seemed to be gallons of a fluid that couldn't be likened to Chanel Number 5. When it was over and all the uproar had ended and peace had descended once again, one very nervous little lady customer asked my mother, 'Does this happen very often?'

Marjorie recalls another story, the story of the friendly (so-called) drunk.

Well, it was Wimpeys who were building the aerodrome in the early forties. They are now a well-known company, but in those days I don't think they were that widely known. Anyway, they employed quite a few Irish labourers and interestingly, for the war effort, quite a few Pakistanis as well. Anyway, our house was on the direct route between where the building of the aerodrome was going on and the local pub the Trusty Servant. We got quite used to hearing all these Irish boys returning from a night drinking session and they boomed out songs like 'Danny Boy' in their lusty Irish tenor voices. But the Pakistani labourers were quite different and subdued by comparison. Because I suppose, probably as a penalty for not obeying the Koran, they could not hold their drink. They got hopelessly drunk.

One winter's night it really was pouring with rain. We were having a family game of Monopoly when we became aware of a most peculiar sound that was rising in volume and filling the house. So we did an investigation and we found that the noise was coming from our own front doorstep. Sprawled in the doorway was a rather tubby, totally drunk, Pakistani, snoring his head off. So we had a little family conference because we didn't really like to leave him there to get sodden with the rain. He was full of beer so we guessed he was sodden already. So we went and got my father's old mackintosh, which he used to cover the batteries for the heating and power for the house, because we hadn't got central heating, we hadn't even got mains electricity. We laid the old mac over the drunk; we didn't feel like touching him really because he smelt rather odd. And then we went to bed.

In the morning our front doorstep was quite vacant again. But then, afterwards, up and until the aerodrome was built, we could see that Pakistani gentleman walking down to the pub in my father's very holey mac. We knew we had done the chap a really good turn!

As we know Marjorie lived opposite Stoney Cross, which of course was an active airfield, so what were her memories of living near such an airfield during wartime?

Well, apart from all the boys who used to come into the tea-room my chief, most vivid memory is, in the wintertime my mother used to fuss as mothers do, that my sister and I were not getting enough fresh air. So, most evenings after supper, we used to walk up the main road until we became level with the main runway, which was within a few yards of the main road. And we used to stand there and watch these great four engine bombers come back in from their missions. The four engines glowed a really deep red and we could smell hot oil and they used to swoop in literally just above our heads. We used to feel so thankful that at least these were some of the boys and crews that had returned safely. That really is my most vivid memory of the airfield in action.

We didn't actually get to visit the airfield because we realised you weren't

A building typical of the sort that was constructed at Stoney Cross. *(Author's collection)*

supposed to, and in those days people were much more law abiding. But security I would have said was very unobtrusive, because I don't think in those days there was the terrorist scares we have in today's modern world. Back in those days, there didn't seem to be that worry and I didn't notice the security. We wouldn't have dreamed of walking on to the airfield, but that was our own discipline.

Of recent times, with all the violence that is around, I can no longer walk as safely in my beloved New Forest. Things like that have made me look back with great nostalgia to those days but I suspect that might just be me looking through rose-coloured spectacles.

As a postscript to her story Marjorie says that she and other locals believe that there is still an unexploded bomb beneath the A31 just opposite the roadside restaurant at Stoney Cross. 'We know that there was a bomb that fell there and failed to explode. No one recalls it being removed at any time and of course the road has been widened and resurfaced many times since the war so it would have been well known if a bomb had been removed.'

12

Through the Eyes of the Children

L ife on the Home Front was difficult at the best of times. Rationing, blackouts, enemy bombing of civilians and much more gave rise to the phrase 'the People's War'. And 'people' also meant children, of course, who viewed the war differently to the adults. Years later many recalled it as an exciting time in their lives. Children of that generation made the most of what they had and despite hardship they only thought about the good times. Life for children in the New Forest had its own difficulties as well as its own rewards.

During the war Jude James was a schoolboy living in New Milton. He is now involved with local history through his work with the New Forest Museum at Lyndhurst.

Jude was very nearly eight years old when war broke out on that Sunday in September 1939. He well remembers the events as they unfolded.

Quite a brilliant early September day it was, with white clouds scudding over. Very peaceful I remember and very calm, given the events which were about to unfold. Actually I suppose, everyone was very anxious that something disastrous was going to happen very quickly, of course little knowing then, that the Phoney War was going to create a period of lull in effect. But, of course, no one knew really what to expect at that time.

Jude lived in Peckham Avenue, New Milton, a small community on the western edge of the Forest, just a mile or so from the coast. His two elder sisters and brothers all eventually went into the services. One sister was later to join the Women's Auxiliary Air Force, his other sister went into the ATS, and served as a member of an ack-ack battery. Jude's eldest brother joined the Army and his other brother the Navy. Happily, they all survived the war. Jude was asked for his most vivid memory of the time.

Well, I think my first, most vivid memory, certainly, is of the bombing of New

Milton, when so many people were killed in the High Street. In fact we'd moved property by that time, and we all lived in Ashley Road, not very far from the main Station Road in the centre of New Milton. And I remember, very clearly, seeing the German bomber overhead. I was playing in the garden and it was early evening time. I was watching the bombs actually fall before I fully realised what was happening. I became a childlike observer of this terrible event, and after it had all happened, although I'd sustained a very minor injury due to broken glass – I'd got a small cut on the head – I went out into the street, and saw the smoke, and the sun through the smoke, very clearly indeed. It was, in hindsight, quite surreal and eerie.

There was a car right at the crossroads in the High Street where the roads go out to Ashley and Stem Lane. The driver was sitting bolt upright. The car was burning furiously and so indeed was the driver. It really was dreadful and that incident from early on always sticks very clearly in my memory, of course. Further up Station Road people from the shops were coming out and putting cloths and blankets and sheets and so on, over the bodies of the dead, or they were helping the injured people as best they could. And the army lorries were going to and fro all this time.

One of my brothers was actually in Station Road when the bombs went off, and the friend he was with, Ian Bryant I think it was, actually suffered quite a severe injury to his leg from the shrapnel that had been flying about. He had to be taken over to Milford-on-Sea Hospital, and the army organised that. I remember him being put on to the back of an army lorry that was in the street at that time. No ambulance was available and this lad was just, I guess, driven straight down to Milford, which fortunately was only a stone's throw away. It all unravelled like a film at the cinema.

So it was a very traumatic period, and the smell of the explosive, the cordite I suppose, whatever was in the explosive, was very, very powerful and I can still recall it in my memory to this day. It was a terrifying introduction to an adult's world, of man killing his fellow man.

Yes, that was all very terrible, but it was a weirdly fascinating event in a way, to witness this destruction and carnage. Today of course people watch this sort of thing every day on TV and they think nothing of it. How times and attitudes have changed.

Looking back, I think the war was very interesting; it was interesting because there were lots of activities and adventure, especially for children. Both the Army and the Navy had a rocket base down the road at Becton for example, and groups of kids used to go down and see these. They used to fire these rockets, I think this was a bit later in the war, out over the sea. There were also some Bofors guns sited down on the cliff top.

Really, all sorts of activities were going on all over the place. So that was quite exciting, but other aspects of the war were very, very boring I am afraid to say. The fact that travelling was difficult and for us children there were no sweets. I mean those were the really bad things, only getting 2 ounces of butter and this sort of thing. We used to buy the half pound packets of butter and they actually had lines drawn round them, three lines, so you could cut exactly into 2 ounce weekly bits. The bread wasn't very good either, I seem to remember. It had no taste at all.

There was a lot of tedium and at school we had air-raid shelters to go into and had practices to do when the raids were on. So there was a great mixture. Some of it seemed endless and tedious, as though nothing was going to happen, and yet it was punctuated by the excitement of being able to talk to soldiers, for example.

People were very friendly in those times and we, as kids, were able to talk to strangers. There was no thought in anyone's minds about this sort of thing and people always helped each other. Soldiers talked to us because maybe we reminded them of the kids they had left at home.

When we were in Ashley Road, Milton, and some of the soldiers just after D-Day were posted near us at Great Ballard, three of them used to come for supper and baths. Actually I think many local people had been asked to provide that facility. One of these chaps stayed for quite a long time and I always remember his first name, Stephen. He used to come and have supper with us and then used to have a bath, and then he would go back off to the camp. I guess this arrangement had been organised by the authorities. So, in those sorts of contacts, it opened up all sorts of opportunities to have new experiences and to meet new people.

My elder sister, when she became a member of the Women's Auxiliary Air Force, had, I suppose, fallen in love with a Polish airman who she used to bring home on leave. So we met people like that and later on of course the Americans came. So there were quite a lot of things that opened one's eyes to so much.

Jude was asked if he noticed a complete change, in the build-up to D-Day, with a lot more troops and activity in the area.

Yes, that was quite remarkable and of course I was that much older and could take more in. I think the importance of what was going on registers much more clearly in one's memory as you get older.

And there were more troops than we had previously seen all around here. I remember in Brook Avenue, for example, there was a whole row of Canadian tanks. These tanks used to go off practising during the day, because one evening, talking to the soldiers there, which we used to do a lot as children, they gave us two of their spent shell cases which they had fired out in the Forest. I took these cases home and my mother polished them up. We had them for a long time, placed each side of the fireplace. I remember they were very heavy to carry. I had to keep putting them down as I was walking home with them. After the war spent shells could be found in scrap yards as well as on the old Forest ranges.

Now further up at Great Ballard there were many more tanks and a little encampment with open tents for the soldiers there. There was a lot of activity at the coast of course, but this area really was out of bounds to us.

I remember hearing stories about, shall we say, local road people, siphoning fuel from the lorries as they waited in line just before D-Day. Not sure if this is true though. They are supposed to have pinched the batteries from the vehicles as well although I would imagine they would have been quite well guarded.

Anyway, it was much more difficult to move about, particularly with the increased police activity. My father and mother were always being asked for their identity cards, if they went on the bus anywhere, to places like Bournemouth, or indeed those places which were in the 'high security' area, which was mainly along the coast. The police would sometimes stop the bus and go through and ask everyone to show their identity cards. So of course one became much more conscious of this. There was, too, a lot more activity in the air. Of course, we noticed the aeroplanes more by then, not only because we were interested

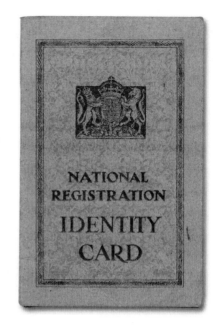

in aircraft, but also because by now they had the new black and white marks painted round their wings and around their fuselage. These had been painted up overnight and they were using them from June 1944 and after for the D-Day Campaign. We also knew most of the German planes – but by then there were not really any about!

As a youngster, interested in the planes, I could identify I think pretty well every one there was. Most kids of my age seemed to have an interest in aeroplanes, particularly the German planes that we learnt to watch out for in the early days. But when D-Day came, we used to say 'There's a Tempest or Typhoon or Spitfire', whatever had gone over. We used to watch them going over usually in great flights across where we lived. Of course, although it was exciting, there was without doubt, great tension that you could sense everywhere. One saw the build-up to D-Day because this area was really crucial to everything they had planned for D-Day. Then when it happened, of course, it came on the news afterwards, and suddenly the place seemed empty. We had seen the men and lorries moving away, but for all we knew at that moment they were going off on another exercise. Looking back, there was certainly an incredible atmosphere. Although you thought you knew what might be happening, nothing was certain until it had been confirmed. That's the way it was and it hit me in later years what a piece of world history I saw unfold in front of me.

Oh, it was very exciting. You see as I said before I was then old enough to begin to follow the war. I remember with the daily paper, we used to take the *Telegraph*, and with the maps that were drawn, we used to assiduously follow the movement of the front line in Europe, fondly believing, as I did as a youngster, that it was easy to just push these Germans back. When it was slow or stopped or we got no news I got very frustrated and anxious about what was happening. But there, that

was that, interest at twelve and thirteen was all about that sort of thing. If nothing
happened or it was going badly, you just lost interest.

Jude was asked about the end of the war – how quickly life reverted back to
normal, in particular in the community in which he lived.

I don't get the impression that it was a very quick process. There were still soldiers
about, and other military people around, for quite a long time. The airfields
continued to function for a while; Holmsley South up on the main road (A31) for
example, continued to be used by the Air Force, as did Beaulieu airfield. They were
bomber bases and had fighters as well. So we still saw a lot of air activity going on.
And it was a kind of, I guess, in hindsight, a winding down rather than a cessation.
From that point of view you sensed the danger had gone, lights were on, and things
then became a little bit easier, but of course rationing continued. Even bread went
on the ration after the war.

So, in some ways, some things seemed more restrictive, in that sense. The threat
of any more danger from the air, or the likelihood of an enemy invasion, had
passed. As I said, there was no more fear of bombing or further raids, or any type of
attack. It was all very slow, it seems quite a dark period on reflection and it's almost
as though one sees it like a black and white film in a curious sort of way. That
dullness, and then the very terrible winter of 1947, which I remember very clearly.
Very thick snow, the railways almost came to a standstill and our buses couldn't get
through. It was good in some respects because we couldn't go to school. I know we

An anti-aircraft crew provides cover for Holmsley South airfield. *(Forestry Commission)*

enjoyed that. It was because the snow was so deep in the Forest for, I don't know, two or three days probably, and the roads were impassable.

Jude still lives and works in the Forest. He is still very much involved with life in the area, but in a different vein. He tells us briefly what he is responsible for now.

Well, my work today is at the New Forest Museum, Lyndhurst, where I'm both the librarian and consultant. Most visitors to the Forest will stop in Lyndhurst and large numbers visit the centre here for information about the Forest, where to go, what to do, that sort of thing. My main function is to try and help the Trustees of the Ninth Centenary Trust to build up a really good museum and resource centre: one which will reflect all aspects of life in the Forest. At the same time, we want to build up a library that is comprehensive, both in books and pictorial material and video and tape material, so that we can provide for the public – quite free of charge – a first rate service for research, reading, and investigation. I feel this is something that has already been partly accomplished and I hope we can really make a go of it in the coming years.

❖   ❖   ❖

Kenneth Robin Hood is a native of the New Forest and his very early childhood was spent in Cadnam. Still a small community today, Cadnam is one of the gateways into the Forest, and thousands of travellers pass through the area every day.

It was interesting for me because my Dad was the local policeman. His name was Hugh Ronald Hood, but naturally he was given the nickname Robin. Whereas I was actually christened Robin, which is rather fun because, like the original Robin Hood, I too have lived in the Forest.

In those days, of course, the police were treated with great respect and I was, I suppose, rather lucky to be the son of a respected member of the community. Of course it meant that I really had to behave myself, more so than the other kids who used to get up to mischief.

I was about nine or ten when the war was announced. We lived in the village police house and Dad was responsible for looking after quite a large area. He used the family car, it was a Ford 10, to get around and I went out with him quite a lot, after school and at weekends. It was exciting but at the time I took it in my stride. It was something that happened and I knew no different.

The events I remember include the evacuees coming out from Southampton and Portsmouth right at the beginning of the war. I remember too the gas masks being issued.

Dad got involved in all sorts of activities to do with movement of people and enforcement of lots of new regulations. This was in addition of course to all his usual duties of looking after community needs and general security and that sort of thing.

He liaised with people from the Army and the War Department and was responsible for some local Intelligence activities. One of the main jobs when there

was a lot of bombing of Southampton and so on was for us to go out and locate
where the bombs had fallen and where aircraft had crashed. Many bombs landed
in the Forest for one reason or another and when people reported these incidents
Dad and I would go and identify the exact locations and he would then report
back to the military authorities. On one occasion, and I remember it vividly, we

went to the site of an aircraft crash. I can't
remember the plane, but it was German
and when we arrived it was still burning
and there were two aircrew inside all alight.
Even though I had to stand well back from
the site, I knew what was going on and the
fact that the pilot and co-pilot had been
burned to death.

On a more light-hearted note, one of the
local farmers rang Dad and said, 'I have a
German pilot sitting in my kitchen eating
breakfast.' The farmer, from the Minstead
area, I can't recall the name, had 'captured'
this chap after his plane landed in one of
the local fields. He was shaken up but
unhurt and so the farmer took him in,
gave him food and called Dad. When we
arrived the German was rather pleased to
see us. He spoke good English and had
visited England before the war. He gave
me a little map as a souvenir. Anyway, we
took him back to the police house and made
arrangements for the military to come and

Kenneth (left) and two of his friends in the
garden of Kenneth's home. *(Kenneth Hood)*

collect him. He seemed a very nice chap.

Like most kids at the time I watched the dogfights overhead and saw the planes
come down, and occasionally the pilots managed to bale out. I went to school at
Copythorne and it was almost opposite that school there was a tea-room, which
was hit by a bomb.

We moved then to Milford-on-Sea because Dad was transferred. Life became
even more interesting because of course that's a village right on the coast and it was
part of the long defence area stretching from Southampton down to Weymouth. But
because it was very close to Southampton and many sensitive military sites, most of
which eventually contributed to D-Day, there were a lot of troops and so on.

My mates, Tom Whittock and John Parker, and I used to visit the AA gun sites.
There were six I think along our stretch of coast. They were Bofors guns and we
made friends with the crews there. They let us play on the guns, gave us refreshments
and we just used to hang around enjoying ourselves. One of my happiest memories
is sitting at one of the sites, drinking tea and eating a crust of bread. For a young lad,

playing at soldiers was a thrilling experience. We knew no fear and did not realise what the war really meant. It was all a great adventure. Some of the local girls would also visit the sites, attracted by the uniforms of the soldiers I'm sure.

Keyhaven was the main catering centre for the sites and was always a good place to visit. All the soldiers were accommodated in bell tents all around the area. One thing that sticks in my mind was the washing facilities for the troops were like the troughs the horses used to drink from. Anyway after a while these things got replaced and we used the old troughs as canoes. They needed a bit of patching up but they were ideal for what we wanted.

One of the jobs Dad was responsible for was keeping an eye on people who were on a special aliens list. I think it also listed people who were not aliens but who were in some way a bit suspect. Earlier, before we moved to Milford, we had to go up to Stoney Cross airfield to check on the many foreign workers who were helping to build the airfield. There were Chinese, Irish, Pakistanis and other nationalities besides. That was interesting to see all these people from overseas. Another job for the police was to sort out the regular pub brawls involving the military and civilian pub customers.

Back to when we were in Milford, I was being taken into school in Ashley, by bus. We had all day school by then because when there were a lot of evacuees in the Forest in the early days, school was a half day for them and a half day for the local kids.

Talking of buses, when the cities like Southampton were being bombed, because the workers could not sleep or were bombed out they were brought out to the

After a raid on Southampton the Cold Storage premises burned for days. (*Hampshire Fire & Rescue Service*)

Forest in double-decker buses which would park up in the trees and these people would sleep out here before returning to work. I remember a lot of buses were always parked on the driveway up to the Bartley Lodge Hotel.

As kids we went into Southampton sometimes and also into Lymington, the nearest big town. I watched a film at the Lyric Cinema in Lymington called *Her Jungle Love* and it featured Ray Milland and Dorothy Lamour.

There were a lot of troop movements in the Forest throughout the war with a good deal of peaking and troughing, until the build-up to D-Day. On one occasion some Canadians had been stationed all around and literally at a moment's notice they were moved. It was quite early in the morning and breakfast had been prepared for hundreds of soldiers. Instead of them getting fed, the cooks came into the village with a truck full of food and told us to distribute it all to the community because the troops didn't have the time or opportunity to eat it. They also left behind six Harley-Davidson motorbikes. Four were later collected but we had two bikes in our shed for ages. I don't know what happened to them.

❖   ❖   ❖

Michael Wright was just ten years old when war was declared on Germany. However, he was prepared, because ever since the events of the Spanish Civil War Michael's father had been telling the family about the inevitability of a war involving Britain.

When war came the family were in some ways relieved, but the parents were dreading the consequences. . . . My father had been saying something like 'Twenty years (after the First World War) and we will be at it again.' Perhaps many of his former Army pals had been saying the same thing, but how uncanny that was.

In 1939 Michael and his family lived in Gosport.

My dad had been in the Royal Horse Artillery and then had joined the Southern Railway. We moved from our home in Gosport when Dad was transferred to the village of Sway. We went into a large rented property in this place, quite a change from the hustle and bustle of Gosport. The area was a delight really because my brother and I could explore the Forest and it was a whole new world of adventure. Up till then the furthest I had been was to Weymouth on a Sunday school outing. We went by charabanc, an old thing even in those days.

I went to St Luke's School. When war came my brother and I thought it all quite exciting. I remember we had some airmen billeted with us. There was a pilot, an observer and one other. Can't remember all their names but I think there was a chap by the name of Pat and another called George.

Sway has a small airfield (ALG) and Michael says he saw an Anson aircraft there.

I think that was my first sighting of a proper aeroplane up really close. You know, a plane that was one of ours, and helping in the war. Oh, by the way, the day the airmen arrived with us Sway was bombed. Most kids were good at aircraft spotting, especially spotting enemy aircraft. Anyway someone thought they saw a Blenheim fly over. I looked up and recognised it as a Junkers Ju88. Peter, my brother, saw it too. It was flying south to north. I called out for Pat who was in the house. He came rushing out and shouted for us to go inside. I was standing transfixed in our front garden.

Anyway, the Ju88 spread its bomb load over the area and I think Meadens Garage was hit or there was a near miss.

Talking about aircraft, I saw Lysanders at Sway airfield. I was later told they were used to drop our agents in France and Germany. I have loved the Lysander ever since.

Another incident I remember very clearly was later when I was going to Ashley School. On my way home on one occasion, as I went across the railway bridge at the New Milton station, I noticed many soldiers standing on the up platform (to Southampton). A few minutes later someone shouted out and everyone was alarmed to see an enemy plane flying low over the railway line towards the soldiers on the station. It was a Messerschmitt 110. It was strafing the railway with cannon fire. The soldiers started firing back and we noticed one of our planes hot on its tail. As the 110 banked up over the water tower it was obvious it had been hit by fire from the chasing plane. It crashed almost immediately over at Mudeford.

As kids, I think you remember the things that as an adult you would want to forget. You know I remember all the crashes, but I don't really remember some of the humorous or day-to-day things, apart from trapping rabbits and getting stuff from the Americans when they arrived. Another time an aircraft crashed at Flexford on an old railway carriage that someone had done up really well and turned into a private home. I was there and saw one of the crew. They were all dead. This one chap had his leg severed. I was with Peter and still to this day he mentions that incident at Flexford. Looking back it was horrible, but at the time we took it in our stride I suppose. Anyway, we took a bombsight from the plane and the next day PC Buntin called at our house. He asked us to return the bombsight we had 'borrowed'. Someone had obviously seen us and reported us, but we didn't get into trouble thankfully. We did learn our lesson though.

When the bombing of Southampton took place us kids stood up at the top of the village, by the Hare and Hounds pub, and watched all the activity in the middle distance. My mother was working on war work at Wellworthys in Lymington and Father, I think, by this time was working in Brockenhurst. I never knew what he did, but he was off the railways and going off every morning to some large house. Occasionally he brought home old maps and we used to play war games on them. There were so many military places in the area by now and we knew Intelligence and other services were very active locally. From time to time soldiers would appear out of the Forest and tell us we should not go any further. I learnt after the war that the underground army was here too.

During the bombings crews were often on duty around the clock. The Salvation Army tea wagon was always a welcome sight. It is seen here in Southampton, *c.* 1942. *(Salvation Army)*

Michael, at the age of twelve, was involved with the fifty-strong complement of the Army Cadet Force in Sway. Their ages ranged from twelve to eighteen and some cadets were issued with Martini rifles. They met twice a week and often at weekends in the officers' house in Brighton Road. The corps was affiliated to the Royal Hampshire Regiment. They provided cyclists, messengers and runners.

We often used to run backwards and forwards to this concrete building at the edge of the village. I was never sure what it was, but some military person was always there to give and receive notes and messages. I used to have a go with the Martini rifle. Because I lived in the country I was already proficient with a twelve-bore shotgun.

After Dunkirk I saw the Red Cross trains passing through the village, then much later I saw some of the first Yanks. They were down at the pub, the Hare and Hounds. I was struck by how big and rugged they seemed.

My friends and I used to visit many of the local airfields. In those days young lads like us could ride off anywhere without fear of strangers. Sometimes we would be gone all day and would visit Holmsley, Ibsley over the other side of the Forest and Beaulieu airfield too. I think it was on a visit to the airfield at Holmsley that the Americans gave us a great big old 28in-frame bike. It had one wheel missing so we walked back home that day dragging the bike with us. We repaired it and had another cycle to add to our transport needs. It must have been one of those RAF issue bikes that maybe they didn't need any more because they couldn't be bothered to repair it. Anyway, it served us well.

Later Michael became an apprentice at Meaden's Garage in Sway. Very few civilian cars were being serviced at that time and the garage was used by the War Department for essential work on military vehicles. Meaden's was also an Army fuel depot, with just one pump for civilian use.

We converted an old 1932 Austin 16 into a fire engine. Just cut down the back end and boarded it over. Nice job, and in those days all sorts of vehicles were being commandeered and used for emergency purposes. . . . Later, in the build-up to D-Day, we worked on vehicles that had sealing material around the engine, you know, around the distributor and plugs and so on. It was for when they went into the water at the beaches. For most of the time we sorted out vehicles from the airfields, servicing, repairs and the like.

Michael's adventures include his visits to the airfields and his time with the cadets:

Going into Lymington, once a week, to get the groceries. We were registered for our supplies at one shop and we had to use that shop at all times. The 8 mile plus trip was always an adventure especially on a bike, carrying the bags on the handlebars. Occasionally we went into Southampton, but that was quite an expedition.

Every village has its local colourful character, and Sway was no exception:

One of the local chaps had never been out of the village in his life. He was summoned to go to the Royal Artillery barracks in London. Upon his return he put it about that when he got to London he thought it was 'market day' because there were so many people about!

There are other things too I think about from time to time. . . . We had an evacuee for a time. His name was Donald, he came from Southampton and he was about my age. He never saw his parents while he was with us, not sure about his family background at all, but he settled with us all right. In the time before D-Day we used to cycle out to see what was happening. In some areas we just couldn't go any further but most times we managed to see what was going on. There were tanks and lorries everywhere. There were trucks at Turnpike and Beaulieu, and the road between Chewton Glen and New Milton was known as Concrete Road for obvious reasons. It was just a massive hard-standing for tanks. We saw tanks arriving on the railway and there was a lot of activity at Core House in the village. We saw bombs travelling on trolleys from the bomb dump up to Beaulieu airfield and we watched aircraft returning, many really shot up, to the local airfields. Early in the war, by the way, I think there were Bofors guns at the Mount in Sway.

13

Cake, Church & Cricket
An Evacuee's Tale

The formative years of a child's life can often contribute to or detract from their future. Evacuation was a traumatic time for parents and children alike, yet many youngsters successfully adapted to the challenge. This is a story upon which one former evacuee reflects many times. From her home on the southern edge of the Forest, Joan Coup talks about a period in her life which has had a profound yet positive effect over the decades since evacuation.

My experience and the experiences of many other evacuees in the village were made happier by the relationships we formed with the local children. We sought out the local kids the minute we arrived at our new schools and while many relationships were casual, others were quite intense. At first it was all very overwhelming, arriving in a strange community with our distinct London accents and the Cornish accent, much stronger than ours, vying to be heard in the confusion and drama that was evacuation. In those days the people who were born and bred in Cornwall stayed in the area because there was ample work and little reason for travelling far. There were only a few examples then of people leaving the area and returning years later with another accent. We soon adapted with villagers and evacuees alike gradually picking up a little of each others' way of speaking.

One of my best friends was John, the son of the next-door neighbour. On rainy days we would play in the hallway of his house with his Meccano set, on other days we would play board games and puzzles on the living room floor in my house. Fine days would see us roaming the fields and the village or playing on the recreation ground. Sometimes we would visit a nearby village called Ladock and en route we were allowed to cross the farm at the top of the hill. We had to go past the barn where the bull was kept so our little group comprising four or five friends would run hell for leather past the barn and over the stile to safety in the field. We shrieked with laughter and marvelled that the bull had not broken free and chased us! Silly really because the animal was very well tethered.

I was never expected to do any chores about the house, although there was a task I was expected to take responsibility for once every week. At the top of our long garden on a large round plinth stood a water pump. Several times during the week the man of the household would have to pump up water into a large tank which stood near the house. On a Sunday it was my turn and I had to pump for 15 minutes and it was the same for the other kids too.

Uncle Sam would ask me if I had done the task and when I replied yes, he would ask again. I later learned that he knew when I was 'fibbing' because he would climb a ladder at the side of the tank and pop his head over the top. He could tell how well I had done by looking at the water level. Those lovely old houses are still there, but the pumps have gone and many of the gardens have been built on.

Another house that still stands is the one which had a huge garden and orchard, with what to us at the time seemed like a very old lady inhabitant. She was Miss Taphouse and every year she would invite half a dozen children to harvest the apples. In return we had a grand tea and were sent home with a large bag of apples which was much appreciated by our host families. As we left, Miss Taphouse would give us her sweet ration. Strangely, we never saw this lovely lady out in the street or at the shops and rumour had it that she never left her house.

The village chapel celebrated its anniversary every year. I belonged to the chapel and attended choir practice, Sunday school, Evensong and the usual Sunday morning service. On the anniversary Uncle Sam would sing in the choir too. I remember the church organ which was hand pumped by a man with one arm. When he got tired one of my friends would take over. My first anniversary was very special. Auntie took me to St Austell to buy a dress and a hat for the big day. I was so excited; buying clothes was a very rare treat and everything was bought using coupons so it was only possible to get clothes when they were really needed. I was decked out in a straw hat with flowers and a pink ribbon, black patent leather shoes, white socks and a lovely pink and white dress. I felt like the bee's knees. This outfit served me well at all the anniversaries I attended at the chapel.

Village children and evacuees all attended the local school, which had only two classrooms. Our teachers, who had come down from London and had lodgings in the village, had to partition each room to be able to teach the various classes. The village recreation ground was used for our playing field which was lucky because there was a swing and a sand pit to enjoy. On one occasion, though, while I was playing in the sand pit, I received a glancing blow from a cricket ball, hit by a member of a visiting team of American soldiers from one of the nearby camps. I was given 2s 6d for my pains, but luckily I was only dazed and no real damage was done. I never played in the sandpit again when the cricket was on!

My stay in Grampound village, near Truro in Cornwall, seemed to me to come to a very abrupt end. One day was much the same as any other, and then there was talk of me going home to London. Before I knew it I was on the station platform saying very emotional goodbyes to my Auntie Florence and Uncle Sam and the many friends I didn't want to be parted from.

I travelled in the care of a local district nurse, Nurse Ballinger who was going to London to pick up a patient for recuperation. The meeting with my mother was very strained we had not seen each other for four years and there were very few letters in between. We were virtual strangers. I do not recall much conversation on the way home. I suppose mum was at a loss like I was.

My brother, Douglas, was at home to greet me in his own childlike way, but I had yet to meet up with my father who was still in the forces. The next few days were rather difficult, but gradually we all relaxed and then it was time for my mother to return to her job in munitions. I started school, but this was very short-lived as the V1 and V2 rockets started coming over and they were very frightening. We also had incendiary raids. I remember when I was coming out of the dentists one afternoon from school and it was almost dark. It seemed to me as though the whole of Crouch End was on fire. I ran home as fast as I could. Some efforts were made to return me to Cornwall because of the raids, but the billeting authority would not allow it. I was sent off to my aunt in Chepstow and it was like being with strangers again. It was all rather upsetting to be honest, with a mixture of shock and surprise. I discovered in later years it was because my aunt was going through a difficult pregnancy, yet in those days I was deemed to be too young to be told of such things. I was well looked after, but not in the same way as my Cornish 'auntie and uncle'.

I stayed in Chepstow for ten months and then returned home to get to know my parents and a new way of life. Again the return home came rather suddenly, one minute I was in Chepstow, the next minute I was on a train. On arrival home I met with my father who was on 48-hour leave for the first time. The next time we met was in a hospital in Chertsey, Surrey. Father had been in an accident and one ankle and one leg were broken. He was there for what seemed like a long time and then he was on crutches with his leg in plaster. He was discharged and was sent home and after that the whole family relationship improved and at last, we all settled down together.

In Cornwall I had become used to fresh vegetables and fresh eggs. I roamed round the wonderful countryside without a care in the world. It was so far removed from the new life I had to get used to in London. Mum was a good cook, but of course food was rationed and like most people we could only eat what was available in the shops. We lived in a first-floor flat and there was no garden to play in. We played on the bombsites and in the streets and we spent a lot of time going to the cinema to the morning or afternoon matinees – sometimes both. Sometimes we would go to the YMCA for our dinner which was 6d for lunch and 3d for a pudding. I would travel on the bus with my brother and another child to Wood Green or Finsbury Park Empire. Very often one of our party would be missing when the bus came to take us home so I returned home minus one and would then be sent straight back to look for them!

I gradually adjusted to my life in London. I could not believe the devastation everywhere. Every street had buildings missing, whole blocks of houses had gone leaving gaps. It was still like that many years later well into the 1950s.

My father by now had been invalided out of the forces and we then managed to rebuild our relationship slowly, but surely. After his demob he eventually had to search for work and before long we were off to a new life in Kent. Here we go again, I thought. However, events during and after the war and my many changes of address I do believe helped to strengthen my character.

My husband and I made many moves during our marriage and I became quite adaptable. During my life I have come up against every emotion imaginable and I

Joan Coup (left).

am sure the strength I gained during my evacuation and the changes bought about
by war, have helped me deal with everything that came my way. And sometimes it
has been unbelievably tough.

As an evacuee I was never short of playmates and the names I still remember to
this day are John, Jimmy, Valerie, Alan, Shirley, Anita, Maureen and Annie. With a
couple of exceptions I have never met up with any of them since I was fifteen and
on holiday with 'Auntie and Uncle'. They've all moved to various parts of the world,
although Alan and I still communicate and meet and Valerie lives in Israel and we
have exchanged visits. I had a very happy and comfortable life during those war
years, not wildly exciting yet safe and loved which was the most important thing.

I sometimes reflect that in retirement here in the New Forest I have found calm
and peace after my many and varied life experiences primarily bought about by the
war. Yet it was from the coastline of the Forest and from the camps and tented cities
all around the area in which I live that many men left for D-Day so that evacuees
like me and everyone back home would have a future. I wonder how their families
coped and what sorrow was bought upon many children of my age who never saw
their fathers again. As an evacuee I saw little evidence of the effect of war on the
Home Front, yet today, within a short distance of my home, I can see reminders
of that time. The remains of some long-forgotten airfields, concrete slipways used
for Mulberry Harbours and derelict buildings once used by the military. Most
poignant of course are the War Graves in churchyards across the New Forest.

I will never forget my childhood as an evacuee. I hope future generations will
take the opportunity to understand how my generation was moulded for better or
worse by war and how we all had to adapt to new situations and often, very sad
and emotional challenges. Our lives in the decades after the war have been shaped
by our formative years and in my case the entire experience was beneficial in the
circumstances. Many youngsters of course had terrible experiences during their
time as evacuees. I feel so sad that they had to endure such upset and heartbreak.

We used to pick up mortars and .303 rounds from the Forest. I, stupidly, put the .303 rounds into a vice in a friend's dad's shed and used to hit them with a hammer. My friend Bill Webb had his hand blown off by a bullet he played with.

14

Breamore:
The Patton Connection

Just north of the Ashley bombing ranges, on the main Fordingbridge to Salisbury road, is the village of Breamore, a preservation area and the country estate of the Hulse family. Like many private estates, Breamore was ideal for the needs of the Army, although they did not arrive here in force until 1942.

While the British occupation of the property was a rather subdued affair, the Americans, by contrast, pursued a more flamboyant policy. Coffee and doughnuts served by attractive young American girls lifted the spirits and made the place seem a little more like home. And the steady flow of young ladies both to the house and to the regular social events held locally also helped to relieve the stresses of military life. No excuse or reason was needed to throw a party or a to hold a dance in the village hall.

Breamore House also served as one of the meeting places for the New Forest Home Guard. Uniquely in this area, the Home Guard was a mounted division whose responsibilities included patrolling acres of the Forest 'in case of landings by enemy Paratroopers'.

Quite what they were supposed to do in the event of such intrusions is unknown, but they were dedicated and no doubt would have fought to the last man had such sacrifice been necessary.

❖   ❖   ❖

Edward Hulse, now Sir Edward Hulse, was a young lad at the time of Patton's arrival at Breamore. He recalls his experience both of Patton and the house during the war years.

What were your earliest memories of Breamore House in the war?

Well really with the English troops here in the house, that would be about 1942. There were an immense number of horses out in the grounds because virtually

Breamore House from the air. *(Author's collection)*

everything was moved by horses in those days. I mean there was the Artillery and the gun carriages and, of course, it was very exciting when you're seven, seeing these very well-disciplined and rather romantic people carrying on in a tradition which I suppose was how they operated years before in the First World War. We also saw the Mounted Home Guard Unit, which operated locally.

How was the house itself put to use by the Army?

Basically, the area that we are sitting in was a map room when the American troops were here. I rather think that it was previously a mess, in other words, a large number of officers came in and ate here when the English were in the house. Remember I was seven at the time so I am not quite certain.

Can you remember the actual divisions or units that were stationed at Breamore?

The English divisions here were, of course, the Artillery, that is the Royal Artillery.

The Great Hall was used as General Patton's office. *(Author's collection)*

Then later, in 1944, we had the Americans. The most outstanding one was, of course, General George Patton who everyone's heard of. He was here for a very short time because Goebbels, the German Propaganda Minister, broadcast the fact that Patton was here and it was then thought prudent to move him on because he was clearly a man of great importance and a potential target for assassination.

The Great Hall, which is open to the public during the summer months, was then a map room and all the maps for Utah and Omaha beach were up in this room. Unfortunately, no one quite knows how, but the Germans were expecting the troops on these beaches and they were probably the two worst beaches as far as casualties were concerned.

But one of the nice things that made life here very interesting was that very small planes, Pipers or maybe they were Austers, used to land in one of the fields called Butcher's Ground which was used as a landing strip during the war. Important generals would arrive by aircraft and, again, that was very romantic to me as a child. We had our own airstrip. Today I don't think any plane could land on it, but of course these small planes could land on very short strips of land.

The atmosphere here around the house in the early days was very optimistic, I have to say it. No one had any idea of the horrors to come, and it was fun here anyway. The Americans were great fun and, for instance, women abounded, there were a large number of women visiting and, you know, all the men had a party. This was very, very different to the situation over at Longford where at General Montgomery's camp they forbade any female company even for married men.

Edward Hulse was moved into the old estate office and used to visit the house from time to time.

I used to come and visit here and there was someone called Colonel Jim Stanford and I used to stay with him. I mean that as a child and the owner of the property I did have access, but always accompanied. It was rather controlled. Outside the windows, for instance, there were sentries, and on the doors there were always sentries. So when I came in here it was always with quite a senior officer.

I think the atmosphere and optimism improved. Yes, it did change, it changed for the better because, it's difficult probably to imagine today, but there was tremendous faith in Patton. He was seen as a genius, a man amongst men. I know that he wasn't popular with some British officers, but for the Americans he was, you know an out and out champion. There was a little incident, a man failed to salute him, he wasn't put on a charge, Patton simply walked across, hit him and he didn't get up. He was a very physical man. He used to drive his jeep as if he was in a race and tore round the village. Everything was rather larger than life.

Are there any other incidents you can recall?

Well, there was a very unfortunate incident when the publican's daughter from the Horse and Groom at Woodgreen got killed in a driving accident. I mean the Americans, they did drive wildly, there's no other comment. But of course they seemed to be above the law . . . you see during the war the authorities did not place the same emphasis on that sort of thing as they did in peacetime. When a soldier committed that sort of offence, it was swept away. It was this unfortunate girl that got killed though.

What was the atmosphere like at Breamore when the English were there?

The English were definitely more disciplined and therefore rather more subdued. They were at that stage, you see, in 1942 when the situation was very tough. We thought we could be suffering an invasion, it really was a little bit more nervous. I suppose the easiest way to describe it is we felt we could be victims or vanquished, whereas there was no doubt that by the time 1944 came things were beginning to turn.

Anyway, in the early days we began to feel that we were the victims. When you

Members of the Home Guard
Mounted Division.
(Sir Edward Hulse)

think of Churchill's famous speech about the victors and the vanquished and there was no doubt that was the feeling. I don't think the atmosphere here was so much to do with having Americans or English, I think it was more to do with the change in time, the change in fortunes from the military point of view.

Moving now to other aspects of life here, the Home Guard for example. Of course, now people laugh about them especially since we've had the television programme, but they were very serious. They were happy people. They always met at a pub for instance, but they still did the job in a professional manner.

The New Forest Home Guard which used to go round and patrol the New Forest to make sure that parachutists didn't land and that there wasn't any infiltration and so on. No, they were a happy group. How effective they would have been, is perhaps another question. They weren't actually based here though. The Home Guard worked on a different basis. They were all around the area and they would have a meet perhaps here or they may have had a meet at the Horse and Groom, which is just across the river in Woodgreen and so on. They all lived in their own houses, they had their own weapons which were in their house at that time, we all kept rifles in those days.

One of the things probably a lot of the young won't realise is that there was no anti-freeze, so that every hour, on the hour, all the tanks started up so that they didn't freeze. This meant right through the night. You could always tell the time because the tanks were being started. They came with the Americans so that's really in 1944 in the build-up to D-Day.

This is a time when security was at its highest. There was of course the great plot to give the Germans the idea that the landings were going to take place at a different location and not at Arromanches. And so that was the time when even I couldn't enter this room, no one without a very high security pass could actually come into this room. You could get into the house, but not actually into this room, the Great Hall.

In 1944 Edward was twelve. How did he view things several years after the outbreak of war?

Oh, I think at that time the propaganda was superb, you believed that the war was over, or almost over. And, of course, you knew the Americans had no rationing. Sweets for example were not a problem for me because the Americans were only too happy to give one candy. So it has to be said aged twelve I was naïve: I believed what I was told and there was this cheerful thing about the belief that it won't be long and we will have won.

Then the house finally cleared of soldiers and equipment, almost as suddenly as it had been taken over. It was eventually handed back in 1947. The main damage done, although it wasn't intentional, was dry rot, believe it or not. The Americans have a very different idea of temperature and they kept this house at about 70°. We try not to have it above 50° and so dry rot was

A war artist's sketch of a Churchill tank near Breamore village. *(Author's collection)*

everywhere. Eventually the insurers refused to meet any further claims and we got some compensation and some insurance. But that was big damage done, and that was the major problem. We were lucky. The house had been let before the war so that the personal goods had been packed up and were in storage. It was very difficult for people who were living in their own houses and were ejected by the military to get their possessions properly packed, because of course everyone in those days was wanting that sort of service. Luckily, we had completed most of the packing and storage.

Was this a halcyon period in Edward's life? Looking back now, many years later, what are his thoughts about what he endured and what he went through?

I think almost everyone's father was away at the war, everyone was in fact therefore brought up by their mother which indeed I was. I think at that sort of age it is a wish to conform and one was exactly the same as everyone else. One had one's friends, one played football and games like that, but particularly football. I was never very good at cricket but it was quite fun. We really got on with it. It was what was happening at the time and I suppose we thought it quite normal. Here we did not really suffer like they did in the big cities and towns, but with the troops here and all the activity, one was only too well aware of how important it was that we

In the years when our Country

was in mortal danger

ERNEST   REGINALD   PONTING

who served from 15 October 1942 to 31 December 1944

gave generously of his time and

powers to make himself ready

for her defence by force of arms

and with his life if need be.

George R.I.

THE HOME GUARD

Members of the Home Guard were officially recognised by the King for their services to their country. *(Sir Edward Hulse)* won the war. It was an adventurous time though and one which remains with you for ever.

With the soldiers, one used to have sort of funny games. They were very good with children. All the children were brought into the house. I remember coming to this room and playing silly games and one was made to stand on one leg and then sort of bending down and someone pushed at the end and we all went flying. It sounds silly now, but one has to remember one was, I don't know, perhaps twelve years old at that time and it was thought terribly funny. And there was no doubt the Americans, in particular, were good with children. They were so far from home and missed their own children, so we were substitutes perhaps.

I didn't come in here for Christmas, though, but that was largely because I was living with my mother most of the time and therefore I was actually with her and her brother at a place called Quinton where there was an Air Force base.

What were Edward's impressions of General George Patton?

Well, as a person he was larger than life. I mean, don't forget, at that stage I'm about twelve years old and he actually looked taller than I know him to be now, so the impression was of someone immensely physical. He was, of course, a great extrovert and he had a great sense of humour and there was an aura around him. Everyone treated him almost as God and so I think I really thought of him as God.

As you know he was rather famous for carrying two pistols and they were very much in prominence. He was I am told a very good shot with them, but I actually never saw him shoot. But the effect was this very physical, strong person, carrying two pistols which no one else did – they all carried one. So he was, you know, that much more important than anyone else. There was no doubt, while he was here, who was in charge.

When he moved about the estate and was out in the grounds he was much less well protected than, say, General Montgomery. One would almost say to a point of carelessness. He really, I think, felt he could protect himself. He was a good shot, he was physically extremely strong and of course there were his own troops everywhere. So, yes, in the house here there were sentries on the door when he was working in this room, but when he went around you would see this jeep, he would very often drive himself as opposed to being driven. And I must say at a really terrifying rate.

After D-Day, there were still people here, but you could tell that the war and our lives were changing for the better. The atmosphere was much calmer and people generally seemed to be in much better spirits. When the house eventually returned to us it was peaceful, like before the war, but life would never, could never, be the same again. It's such a long time ago now that when we walk around the house and grounds it seems as though it never actually happened. With Patton here and the contribution that the house made to D-Day it is quite an historic site, but today it seems like a film or perhaps a dream one might have had.

15

A Soldier Remembers

From the New Forest to the battlefield of Europe, one man's reminiscences tells it all. The memories transcribed here belonged to William Tandy, who joined the Royal Artillery on 29 July 1940. He then transferred to the RAOC on 16 March 1944 and was demobbed from the Army on 2 June 1946:

The following extracts from Tandy's reminiscences are included by kind permission of the Tandy family.

Bill Tandy. *(David Tandy)*

It was August 1939 and with the war very much in the air, I too was very aware of it, as I had been building gun pits and roadblocks. The main road was very busy with military equipment, and getting busier, day by day. Then came that fateful day, September 3rd, it was a Sunday. I had been working on road markings, when at 11 o'clock Prime Minister Chamberlain told us we were at war with Germany. Now for quite a long time things stayed as they were. That was until late September. Then we began to see spotter aircraft appear at great heights, I think about 25,000 feet. On a clear day, I could spot the plane, it was about the size of a blackbird. As it got closer, it would meet with ack-ack fire, but this aircraft was just too high to reach. Barrage balloons could be seen 20 miles away and I was aware that the day was coming when I would be called up for military service. The black-out came into force, which made the winter seem even bleaker. I was still working on the war effort for the Highway Department building defence pits, road blocks and painting lamps for Air Wardens. As the winter passed into spring, things began to happen. The war was not going well on the Western Front as Germany was by now expanding its grip all over Europe. Then later, came the evacuation of our forces from Dunkirk.

The County Council formed an Engineers' Regiment and asked for volunteers, so I went for my medical, however, I did not pass as A1, so I was not accepted. I carried on with my work until I was called up when my 'papers' came. I was told to report to Lyndhurst, in the New Forest, Hampshire. This was of course a nervous time for me, as I had never been so far away from home before, even though I was married with a young son of three years old. The parting at the railway station was a really sad affair and that day I remember especially well, it being 29 July 1940. As the train left the station we all waved until we were out of sight of our loved ones.

I embarked on a train for Southampton. I was already feeling very lonely because I knew no one. I suppose everyone felt the same. Eventually I arrived at Southampton station at 2 o'clock in the afternoon. As I departed from the train, I was aware that there were many men like me all going to the same destination. It wasn't long before we all got chatting and found we had come from all walks of life. We all had to change trains for Lyndhurst Road station and on arrival there we were met by a fleet of army lorries. We departed through the New Forest and through the town of Lyndhurst to the hotel called Cuffnells,* and arrived by tea-time. Of course the hotel was not our quarters, we were in fact billeted in tents under cover of the trees surrounding the hotel. It had been a long day so it didn't take long for all of us to get to sleep.

We were woken the next day at 6 o'clock. The day had broken a fine sunny morning. After shaving and washing, and being given a very welcome breakfast (still dressed in our civilian clothes by the way), we were lined up to be introduced to and addressed by our army captain and sergeants. After this, we were paraded to collect our uniforms, eating utensils, bedding and rifles. The rifles dated back to the First World War but had originally been designed in the nineteenth century. We were paraded again and then we were told that we were joining the Territorial RE at Southampton.

In the weeks that followed our arrival we were on our basic training and drills. As time went on, we began to learn a lot more about each other, and believe me there were some 'queer' ones amongst us. There were chaps from all over England

---

* Cuffnells was once the home of the Hargreaves family. As a little girl Alice Hargreaves (née Liddell) was the inspiration for Lewis Carroll's 'Alice' in *Alice in Wonderland*. Two of her sons were killed in the First World War, Captain Alan Hargreaves DSO in May 1915 and Captain Leopold Hargreaves in September 1916. Alice is buried in Lyndhurst church, on the hill at the top of the High Street.

Bill Tandy and friends somewhere in France. *(David Tandy)*

and in time the army could do nothing with some of them. For example, one became a conscientious objector and knelt and prayed outside his tent all day. Others rebelled in training so that not much could be done with them and some even rebelled against military service. In time they all disappeared from the unit.

It always seemed to be such beautiful weather, but the training was hard, with physical exercise and route marches through the forest, 5 or 6 miles at a time, sometimes in full battledress. We saw many enemy aeroplanes overhead and heard the ack-ack guns firing at them, but they were mostly too high and out of range. Later, in September, air fights were getting more intense with many more air raids at night. By this time though, we were coming to the end of our training. At the end of 8 to 10 weeks, we were split up into units to be put on sites all around Hampshire. Just before this happened, we had an air raid that took place in the daytime. This was our first experience of the screaming bombs and they fell all around us in the forest and the Lyndhurst area. Some bombs had delayed timing, so of course we were called in to help with filling sandbags that would be placed around the bombs and the buildings where they were. One bomb went through the Fire Station roof and through the seat of a chair leaving a perfectly round hole in the seat and then buried itself in the floor. This one did not go off. Later on after the bomb had been defused, both the chair and the bomb were on display for all to see.

I had by now started driving lessons on a lorry made locally at Southampton at the Thornycroft* works and after just six weeks, I passed my test. Our group was made up into a searchlight unit to occupy different sites around the area as required. Then came a scare, because we were quickly mustered, then told that an airborne invasion was on its way to the south coast. We were all sent to 'defend' the Bournemouth and Southampton railway line. This only lasted for four days and nights; however, we had been told that we would have to defend it to the very last man because there were no replacement troops available! When things became quiet and the apparent invasion was not going to happen, we returned, with considerable relief, to our base. When you think about it we didn't have much of a chance because all we were issued with was the First World War rifles and a few machine guns.

Air raids increased night and day and we all moved to various sites around Southampton although I stayed in the forest, at Brockenhurst, which became the first site where we were on our own. The unit numbered just ten, including a cook.

* Thornycroft also had premises in London and Basingstoke. They were the largest manufacturer of military vehicles and related products for the war effort. They are perhaps best remembered for the postwar ANTAR heavy tractor unit. They became part of British Leyland and then AEC, and eventually disappeared as truck manufacturers in their own right. Vosper Thornycroft remains the flag bearer for this legendary organisation.

The unit was operated by the Number 1, who was the corporal, numbers 2-3-4-5 who were the sound locators, numbers 6-7-8 were the projector operators and number 9, and that was me, the generator operator. This was a lonely job because I was located 300 yards from the rest of them really to avoid them suffering from the interference of the generator. So when we were in action, I was on my own unless or until the cook from the cookhouse brought some food down. In the September and October, when the battle of Britain was on, a lot of the action took place over our area. Dogfights and bombers every day, with the German bombers and fighters outnumbering our planes by maybe ten to one at that time. You see, we were near the Solent, just opposite the Isle of Wight, and all the enemy raiders coming to attack inland came over us, both coming in and returning afterwards. We were manning the gun pits 24 hours a day and raids were increasing daily. So in October when the nights were drawing in, we were on duty from 6 o'clock in the evening till midnight, then starting again at 2 in the morning. This went on for weeks on end with searchlights blazing and the ack-ack guns firing. We got very little rest during this time. Also, it was dangerous to walk about because shrapnel was falling around us, because of the bombing.

Usually, when a German bomber was hit with the ack-ack guns, the bomber would release any bombs left on board and these would drop anywhere. Our morale at this time was not very good I'm afraid because like a lot of the chaps I had not been home since joining up in July, and it was now November.

I was then moved to a new site at Exbury, really out in the wilds on a farm. They were very good to us and in our free time I would walk round the farm talking to the farmer and watching the sheepdogs rounding up the sheep. The farmer told me that he trained dogs that were sent abroad to Australia and New Zealand to work on the farms there. He had also trained a dog, called Bob, for a film.

One night in December, the 5th to be exact and the night before I was due to go on leave (it had been six months now and I was looking forward to it), an alert came through on the short-wave radio telling us that a wave of bombers was coming over the south coast and heading our way. This was 6 o'clock in the evening and sure enough they came and were first engaged over the Isle of Wight and then by the coastal batteries. They made their way towards Southampton and Portsmouth, and were chased all over the skies by searchlights. It was murky weather. Suddenly one of the bombers got in the beam of a searchlight and it really stood out like a seagull. It let its bombs go, the first a mile away in a straight line up the Beaulieu river. The bomber kept on heading for us, dropping its bombs all that way, with each bomb getting closer by the second. Also every second it dropped three, so I thought the next ones would hit the farm and us. Well, as it turned out that one bomb fell near the farm, and the plane must have veered off slightly because the rest fell away from us. I rang the rest of the unit to find out how they had fared only to learn that they took evasive action by jumping into the defence trenches. They found that these trenches were full of water and nearly got drowned. Afterwards one of them said to me, 'I'd sooner get drowned than blown to bits'.

It was 2 in the morning before the all-clear came and that didn't give me or the others much time to get ready for our first leave on 6 December. I didn't sleep much after that terrible night and by 6 o'clock I made my way to the cook wagon and had breakfast. Then we waited for the ration truck from HQ to bring in the rations and take us leave personnel back to HQ for money and leave passes. This was some 14 miles away and we had no idea that anything was wrong at HQ. As instructed, we had kept in touch with HQ every 15 minutes, all through the night. The lorry driver then told us that a bomb had dropped in the middle of the HQ site at a place called Bunkers Hill near Pikes Hill and to the northern part of Lyndhurst. We said neither we, nor HQ, had missed a call all night. The driver replied that the radio operator had spent the whole night under a table to protect himself so as not to cause panic around all the various sites that he was in contact with. We then learned that one crew member had been killed and several had been wounded. We then made our visit to several sites and then to HQ and we could all see for ourselves the extent of the damage. In a butcher's shed I saw where a piece of shrapnel had gone through twelve steel dishes stacked one on each other.

I collected my money and leave pass and made my way home via Romsey and Salisbury. My short leave came to an end, and I was soon back at camp. Things were much the same as before, the battle for the air being won, but the raids were increasing so it was not a very good Christmas. The New Year (1941) was not much to look forward to, because with raids every night and day we got very little sleep and that made everyone fed up. As the nights opened up things began to happen. We were moved to a new site at a place called Soberton.

This was well into the countryside so we had more time to relax in the daytime. One summer's evening, a farmhand came up to us with his shotgun and asked if

Somewhere in France, 1944.
(David Tandy)

I wanted to go rabbiting with him. We were all standing at the back of the cookhouse at the time. I turned round, at the same time heard a shot being fired, and found I had been hit in the back by this chap with the shotgun only 10 feet from me. I felt numb but managed to run into my billet and grab a towel to put around my back at waist level and fell forward on to my bed. My mates, having seen what had happened, came to me and on the transmitter summoned an ambulance. This took a long time as it was 8 o'clock before I left for the hospital. The chap with the gun went off and shot a rabbit. He then brought it back to the billet, and asked if we wanted it. My mates and the doctor gave him such a dressing down. I bet he remembered this event for the rest of his life. I was sent to Netley Hospital, Southampton. By 9 o'clock the numbness began wearing off and the pain was getting unbearable. First to an x-ray room, then the operating theatre. It was the early morning when I came round. I was very lucky, as the pellets had spread over a wide area with a long scar. I couldn't move and at nights the air raids were still heavy with bombs falling all around us. Those cases that could walk went down to the shelters, but I could not be moved, so I had to stay put in my bed. It was very frightening, but we didn't get hit. This hospital was beautiful except it was built nearly all of glass and was a quarter of a mile long. They used to drive jeeps up the long corridor. I'm told the reason was a mix-up in the plans. This one should have been built in India and the Indian one here! I remained here ten to fourteen days and was then transferred to Battle Hospital over in Reading. Recovery speeded up and eventually I went for walks outside in the grounds and in the park and by the river. After two weeks I went home for ten days, but I was restricted in the way I could turn.

I returned to my unit. Things were changing in that we were formed now into a cluster; that meant that three sites had been made into one. So for me it meant that I was no longer on my own because now there were three generators together. This made a greater cluster of projectors. Time was arriving for a new piece of equipment called ESL that was driven by power instead of the old method of human hearing. Days got longer with spring, and the nights were shorter, giving us more rest. In the daytime dogfights still took place and we were still outnumbered in the air. Our fighters were splitting up the German bombers and this was putting them off their targets. We carried on our duties just the same. I went on a course to become a driver mechanic at the Battery HQ. This covered both practical and theory to make me a licence holder. One day whilst in the classroom I remember the day was dull and misty with the clouds low. About 11 o'clock we all heard an aircraft and at once recognised it as a German bomber: they sound quite different to our aircraft. It was very low and now it suddenly came out of the clouds that did scare us a bit. Our instructor just carried on with the lesson. At 12 o'clock the bomber was over Totton and by 10 past 12 it had dropped its bombs on the Burts

* It is unlikely that the aircraft had been circling for one hour because this would have left it vulnerable to attack by one of the many AA batteries or fighters in the area at the time.

and Harvey Tar Distillery there. Not one person was injured. At the time it was said 'Why did the bomber fly round for that hour before dropping its bombs?'* Locals who worked at the tar works reckoned that the pilot must have been a crew member off some of the German ships that came to the tar works before the war. The pilot must have known it would be lunchtime there after 12 o'clock. He had waited for all the workers to go to lunch.

Well, I passed my trade test as a driver mechanic. That gave me an extra sixpence a day and I was entitled to wear a badge of a steering wheel on my left arm. This once obtained, whichever branch of the Army you are posted to, no one can take that away from you or stop you wearing it on your left arm. I returned to my unit again back on more training and guard duties – that was for 24 hours a day consisting of 2 hours on and 4 hours off. We did get more leisure time and managed to play football and write letters, but not much time for anything else. The longer summer nights gave us more time. I took a lorry and a mate down to a stream or ford that ran across the road at a place called East Meon to wash the lorry. Whilst there in our Wellington boots, we walked down the stream which was about 12 inches deep. My mate suddenly said, 'There's a trout in here', and sure enough there was. So he said 'Get a bucket and catch one'. I said 'How?'. He said, 'Let's tickle one and flip one out on the bank.' He walked in the stream, I on the bank. He walked for about five minutes carefully, while I watched him with interest, never having seen it done before. With a quick flip suddenly a trout was on the bank, then another and another until we had six. Back at camp our mates weren't interested and would not eat them as they said they aren't good for you. Well, not coming from the countryside they didn't know. They all came from towns and cities like London and the like. So my mate and I had a feast all to ourselves. This is a lovely part of Hampshire and our sites are all over it. We even had one on Hythe Pier on Waterside. We had weekly courses at HQ and my job with the lorry was to pick up various troops for these. I travelled 60 to 80 miles per day over various routes. We used the generator lorries for this work.

It is now 1942 with heavy raids on both Southampton and Portsmouth and of course up country. So, being on the south coast opposite the Isle of Wight, we were in line of all raids inland. We engaged the bombers when they came in and then hours later when they returned for home. The country had been split into zones, fighter zones and gun zones. We were in a gun zone so you can imagine how concentrated we were. So on a heavy raid the flack would be flying everywhere and with the lorries on full throttle you could not hear what was going on. In the fighter zones the fighters had the freedom to seek out the bombers and destroy them. Sometimes there was confusion when our bombers returned from a bombing raid over Germany and were limping home sometimes only on one engine. They would, and did, on occasions get mistaken for the enemy, and were engaged. That was, until one of the crew dropped the colours of the day in the form of flares that changed twice daily. It could be, say, Red Red Green so then we would disengage and take the beam away. It wasn't unheard of for a German bomber to follow one of ours to where ours would land and then drop bombs on the runway. By 1943 our air fighters were increasing in numbers, so air raids were less, as our fighters got the upper hand. With fierce dogfights and splitting up of the German formations, they could pick the bombers off one at a time. It was good to see this. We now began to realise the Battle of Britain was being won. By the end of the year things got so easy so that one battery of each regiment was to be disbanded, and sent to be re-formed into units for the second front. The rumours turned out to be true, and so at Christmas the regiment got together for the last time. After Christmas we were told that the last battery in each regiment would go. As I was in the 394 battery that was the last one after the 391. We hung around a bit till we knew where we were going.

I found that being a tradesman I was going to a motorised unit. This was to be the RASC. We went out most days to learn convoy work and the correct distances between each vehicle. It was obvious we were preparing for the second front. It was now March 1944, with the Battle of Britain won and our home defences very much modernised. It was now easier to detect enemy aircraft so the numbers shot down increased. The enemy struggled to reach targets here and had to find other methods to reach us. We learned later they were using the flying bombs that required no personnel to fly them.

We were still increasing in strength and went to the Ordnance Depot and took delivery of Dennis lorries, 6 tonners they were. Our unit became the 714 Company of Heavy Transport. We moved first to Worksop near Nottingham then on to Weybridge in Surrey. Here, in the countryside, under plenty of cover, in the next few weeks all types of regiments joined us. These consisted of bicycle units, tanks and heavy guns. We had no doubt that we were the second front, especially as we had to learn to waterproof our lorry engines. We did everything necessary to stop the water entering the engine and any breathers. To test our lorries we went to a gravel pit nearby that had been especially adapted for us. We driver mechanics with a sergeant instructor from a special unit took part in the first trials on two different makes of vehicles. There was a concrete ramp going down into the pit and one the other end with about 100 yards of water between at about 5 feet in depth. The drill was to put the truck in low gear with your foot off the throttle and continue slowly down the ramp until the truck hit the water. Then to give the truck full throttle and then carry on out the other side. The first driver and truck went in, but the truck just floated and because the wheels had not even touched the bottom, it had no means of propulsion. We were instructed to take the inspection cover out in the back of the truck and for four of us to get in the back as well. As soon as we hit the water, and the level reached the top of the lorry's door, the water came in the back. We all found ourselves up to our waists in water. Anyway this did the trick and was a success.

Anyway, after that, we travelled by rail back to Bristol. As it was daylight, I could see that if I got off the train before Temple Meads station, I could save myself a 6-mile trip back to my home. So with a swift goodbye to my mate, I opened the carriage door and jumped down to the track. It was a long way down, but I was OK, and walked along the track to Patchway station where there was no one about. I left and went up on to the main road where I got a lift and was at home for 9 o'clock. At 10 o'clock a telegram came saying to return immediately to my barracks. I said to my wife, well they can wait, I'll go back this afternoon. So I made the best of the time and had lunch. I stood outside to wait for a lift. After only 5 minutes, a lorry stopped and with goodbyes to my wife I was on my way back. I enquired where the lorry was going and was told Carlisle. As I was going to Crewe, the lorry driver said he would drop me off at Newcastle-under-Lyme that was only 20 miles from where I wanted to go. I got to the barracks at 6 o'clock that evening. The sergeant said he didn't expect me until tomorrow! The next day I was to go for a medical at Chester hospital. I was woken at 6 o'clock and was on the bus by 8, went to the hospital, had the medical and returned to the barracks, only to be told by the sergeant that I could have a 24 hour leave if I wanted it. Having thanked him, I was off, but had to pay the train fare myself this time. It was good to be home, but the day soon passed and I was back at the barracks again.

As 1 June approached, things began to happen: first the tanks went, then the heavy guns. On 3 June we went in convoy to London, to be met by a police patrol which escorted us around London to Epping Forest, where they left us. We carried on to Wanstead Flats and on to the big common that had a large brick wall, 6 foot high, all round. Through the centre of this enclosure was a road with large gates on either end. We were all directed into here to find the whole place full of every conceivable piece of Army equipment. Some of our mates said, 'Now they got us in here they'll never let us out.' Later that day we all changed our money to Francs so we knew where we were going, but not when. That evening we were entertained by show business stars. Next day, the 4th, we were busy taking all of our lorries and equipment down to the Royal Albert Docks and loading on ships; ours was called the *Ocean Vengeance*. All units loaded that day and at the end we were transported by double-decker buses back to the Wanstead Common area to wait around.

It was at 6 o'clock in the evening, on 5 June, that the double-decker buses arrived and took us back to the docks. On our way there, the public would be saying to each other, 'What a lot of troops. I wonder what they are up to?' We knew. We boarded with all our kit and at about 8 o'clock, a lot of us were looking over the side to the dockside. There was a police sergeant looking up. I won't forget his words to us. 'Good Luck My Boys', he said, with his helmet raised. 'I know what it's like – I've been there myself.' The ship slipped its mooring, and we made our way down the Thames.

We halted about a mile off the shoreline on 6 June. This was also one of the roughest June days for forty years, so we floated here and waited to be taken off by the Americans with their landing craft.

Epilogue:
The Legacy Lives On

The National Park Authority has been in existence since 2006 and through its actions it is championing the interests of the New Forest through partnership, innovation and co-ordinated working to achieve three key objectives.

While much of the landscape we see today has been shaped by man over many thousands of years, the impact of both the world wars and in particular the Second World War has strongly influenced parts of the National Park's character. This takes the form of surviving and very visible structures such as air-raid shelters and ancillary units to major installations including former airfields and bombing ranges. All these have left evidence in the landscape which in some instances is best viewed from the air.

Much of the landscape was returned to its pre-war use and to achieve this often involved the total removal of some features. Other post-war activities such as gravel quarrying in the Avon Valley have removed most of the airfield evidence at Ibsley for example, though fortunately some of the associated structures survive including the control tower. Wartime buildings were once quite common place across the country, but increasingly are now seen as rare survivors and as monuments to a particularly important part of this nation's history. As such many believe that these remains should be given Listed Building or Scheduled Monument statutory protection. The prime objectives of the National Park Authority are to conserve and enhance the unique environment of the National Park, and in particular the special qualities of its landscape, wildlife and cultural heritage, to encourage everyone to understand and enjoy the National Park's special qualities, while ensuring that its character is not harmed, and finally, to support the social and economic well-being of local communities in ways that sustains the National Park's special character

The New Forest National Park through its various roles can strongly influence the retention of some wartime structures through negotiation with land managers and landscape management agreements. As a planning authority and through planning conditions for development, the National Park is now requiring detailed records to be made where it is not possible to retain wartime structures. Future generations will at also be able to appreciate, through drawings and photographs, those buildings and structures that cannot be preserved. Many wartime temporary military buildings often found new uses after the war and were moved to new sites. Some were converted to domestic use and are now often at the end of their useful life and cannot be further adapted. Again as part of the authority's planning

Air raid shelter at Bisterne recently
recorded. *(NFNPA)*

requirements, detailed records prior to demolition will be required.

There is a real need to improve our knowledge about the types and location of wartime structures so that correctly informed decisions are made about their future. The National Park is working to enhance the publicly available record and archaeological field survey and routine site visits are now locating Second World War structures and air-raid shelters that have not previously been recorded. Detailed archaeological surveys of the New Forest coastline and the maritime environment, part of a major national project, should increase our knowledge of coastal installations. Recent work, for example, has located previously unrecorded Luftwaffe aerial photographs taken for the German U-boat or submarine division of the Kriegsmarine. These cover the Lymington and Southampton Water areas and provide very clear indications of many wartime sites.

Similarly, basic research in the national and other archives indicate that there is a vast amount of documentation available for research. These once top secret

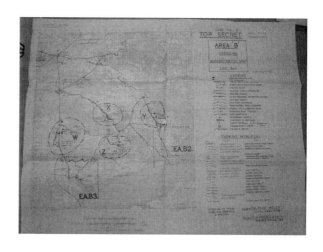

Example of Operation Overlord
map *(National Archive: Picture by
Richard Reeves)*

documents associated with Operation Overlord and D-Day are publicly available and there is a very real need to establish the range and quantity of this material. This could provide a greater insight into the use of the forest for a whole range of wartime activities including previously secret activities.

The Second World War is sufficiently long ago and is increasingly the subject of public interest and research. Fascinating insights into how institutions and people managed their lives and work during the war period needs to be recorded. Examples of new information are almost a daily occurrence. While it is generally known that the larger country houses were used by the military as operational bases, as hospitals and for institutional purposes, many smaller houses quite often functioned in the war effort as locations to store important collections from our national museums. Other details are poorly understood, however. For example, a large contingent of Irishmen engaged in building the Mulberry Harbours on the Cadland Estate had to be housed and fed locally. How was this achieved?

It is vital to continue to promote and facilitate local oral history projects to provide information and this is seen by the National Park as highly important, not only to understand local and long-term traditions, but also to gain personal stories of people's views about the war years. Quite how they managed with rationing, what their memories of bombing raids might be, what they did in any spare time,

Valley View, Woodgreen near Fordingbridge, part of a Second World War Army barrack hut. *(NFNPA FG)*

or quite simply how the war changed their lives for the better or worse.

Those who had families living and working in the New Forest during the Second World War have stories to tell, some of us have them first hand and others through family members. They can all provide human interest. It could be as simple as the Royal Marine unexpectedly being given leave, turning up on Christmas Eve only to be told he would have to find another chicken if he expected to eat Christmas dinner. An ultimately successful, though protracted negotiation over a one-legged chicken took place with a local farmer in Brockenhurst has become a family story.

We should not forget that the war brought people together for the first time from very differing social backgrounds, through their work for example or through being billeted or lodged as evacuees. City children often found their first taste of country living and the freedoms and adventures they could have in the forest both exhilarating and daunting.

A priority has to be the collection of as many of these stories as soon as possible through parents and grandparents before memories are lost. The National Park, by bringing groups and individuals together is keen to facilitate protecting the wartime legacy for educational and long-term historic benefit. Visitors and residents in the future would then be able to appreciate the sites and the part played in the war effort by the New Forest, enhanced by the human interest stories individuals still have to share.

❖   ❖   ❖

The beauty of the Forest has survived the harsh realities of war and provided an oasis in a modern world, inspiring poets, writers and artists. The past, however, continues to present itself.

On a crash site some miles north of Stoney Cross, away from the road between Brook and Godshill, small pieces of debris from an Albemarle lie strewn over the Forest floor. During a parachute exercise the aircraft got into difficulty and fell to earth. The crew was killed. While the wreckage of the aircraft was removed at the time it remains through fragments of glass, metal, wood, screws and other items, which can still be retrieved from the site.

There are other places, too, where the keen observer can find small fragments of crashed aircraft. After sixty years or more it is almost as though the spirit of these men and their machines refuse to leave this world, for to do so may mean we forget the sacrifice of a generation.

On a more practical and happier note, despite the passing of the years many original wartime buildings are still in use. Examples include the clubhouse at Hurn, now Bournemouth International Airport, and Blister hangars at Pylewell and Crow near Ringwood. The latter was moved from another part of the Forest to accommodate the New Forest Owl Sanctuary.

There are many derelict wartime buildings still scattered around the Forest and these include the former Squash Court and Powerhouse at Holmsley South,

A veteran meets his modern-day counterpart. *(Author's collection)*

situated on private land just off the main A31 on the road to Bransgore. On the same road are kerbstones which denote one of the entrances to Holmsley, and just beyond that are two Maycrete buildings now occasionally used as stabling for horses. Further along the road is a concrete airfield track disappearing into the trees, and in the adjacent woodland there are a number of blast shelters. Not far away is the former Command Centre that was used to direct operations in the Bay of Biscay.

The most recognisable of the derelict buildings remaining in the Forest is the Control or watchtower on the site of former RAF Ibsley, near Fordingbridge, which is now a private nature reserve managed by the local water company. The tranquil setting here is very much a fitting tribute to those who served at Ibsley and especially to those who gave their lives for freedom and peace. They are also remembered on two memorials, one of which is sited at what was the end of the

A typical Maycrete building of standard design as used on airfields. *(Graham Buchan-Innes)*

A typical Maycrete building, as found on wartime airfields. *(Graham Buchan-Innes)*

Ibsley memorial stone.
(Author's collection)

main runway at Ibsley.

Traces of Advanced Landing Grounds, often in use for no more than a few months, are more difficult to find. Various USAAF and RAF fighters were dispersed around these ALGs. Crews lived in tents or huts and enjoyed little more than basic conditions. Hazards on these hastily created military sites were many and varied. On many occasions aircraft were prevented from taking off or landing because of the poor weather on these very exposed sites or because of animals on the airfield, as we have heard before. Little can be seen of the Advanced Landing Grounds at Winkton and Bisterne. Deep underground on part of the Winkton site is a relic of the Cold War. A regional seat of government for use in the event of a nuclear attack, a huge three-storey bunker, is now being used for document storage.

Few of the many thousands of people who arrive at and depart from Bournemouth International Airport are aware of the history of the site. Originally known as Hurn, it was the UK base of, among other units, the USAAF 397 Bomb